PETRIFIED CAMPUS
The Crisis in Canada's Universities

David Bercuson

Robert Bothwell

J.L. Granatstein

Random House of Canada

Published in Canada in 1997 by
Random House of Canada Limited, Toronto.

Canadian Cataloguing in Publication Data

Bercuson, David Jay, 1945-
Petrified campus: the crisis in Canada's universities

Includes index.
ISBN 0-679-30876-8

1. Education, Higher - Canada. 2. Universities and colleges - Canada.
I. Bothwell, Robert, 1944-   . II. Granatstein, J.L., 1939-   . III. Title.

LA417.5.B473 1997   378.71   C97-930904-2

Printed and bound in the United States of America.

10 9 8 7 6 5 4 3 2 1

For Robert Craig Brown
Teacher, Colleague, Friend

Contents

Acknowledgments

Our research has been greatly assisted by Melina Ivkovic and Gail Corbett. They have checked data, searched for obscure books and articles, and worked diligently on our behalf. We are most grateful to them and, though tempted, cannot take the opportunity to blame them for any errors that may remain — those are our fault.

Chapter 1

Canada's Universities:
Still on the Road to Ruin?

IN THE EARLY FALL OF 1984 a small, blue-covered book appeared in bookstores across the country. It was called *The Great Brain Robbery: Canada's Universities on the Road to Ruin*. We wrote it. It caused a sensation among university administrators, faculty members, students, and faculty associations and unions. Its message was simple: Canada's universities were, on the whole, not very good and were getting worse with each passing year. It was a polemic. It was short; only 160 pages. It was punchy: one chapter was entitled "Tenure Is a Four-Letter Word." It was irreverent. Some of its readers also thought it was funny. Many of the people who taught in Canadian universities didn't think it was funny at all.

Most books written about higher education are thick tomes with hard covers and hundreds of notes. They get read by a number of university presidents and vice-presidents, a few score of deans, a handful of higher education faculty, and no students. Most university libraries have many of these books. They are serious studies of an important subject and they ought to be treated with respect. But they have little immediate impact on public policy precisely because they are scholarly tomes and almost no one takes notice of them, especially scholars.

The Great Brain Robbery wasn't of that ilk. It was designed to shake and to shatter idols. It was meant to stimulate public debate on the nature, quality, and direction of higher education in Canada and on the public's right to know what was going on in the ivory towers that they, after all, pay for. We wrote it to stir things up. We believed that if university professors were not prepared to debate the merits or drawbacks of tenure, unionization, curriculum reform, or anything else that made up the Canadian system of higher education — or not willing to admit that their colleagues had a right to do so — then Canadian higher education was living a lie.

If universities are to teach students how to think, how to use their brains, rather than to cram facts into them, then universities must also be places of free inquiry. Free inquiry is the simple freedom of professors and students to seek after knowledge, truth, beauty, even ugliness, wherever they believe they may find it. It is the freedom not to be constrained in research, teaching, or the distribution of ideas by preconceived notions of ideology or other limitations. There are always limits on *any* freedom, but in a university the default drive must always be free inquiry.

That is an ideal, and we show later in this book how that ideal is coming under strong attack from a number of quarters. But we still believe in free inquiry, and we believe that it must begin at home, or it is a hypocritical freedom at best. Good journalists know they must not give in to the "Afghanistan syndrome" — the temptation to write critically and analytically about everything in the world except what is happening in their own neighbourhood. It doesn't take much moral courage to write a story about the way the government of Afghanistan, for example, is destroying civil liberties in that country. But it does take courage to write a story about the way the local school board may be persecuting a teacher for being gay. If we can't do the latter, we have no moral right to do the former.

When we wrote *The Great Brain Robbery*, we thought the same principle ought to apply to the ideal of free inquiry in universities. We still do. It's easy to analyse Karl Marx, or discuss the foreign policy of the United States, or even to teach that William Shakespeare didn't really write the plays attributed to him. It's difficult to proclaim that tenure is a protector of lazy and incompetent professors, or that grade inflation is eroding the value of a university degree. Our colleagues won't much care what we say when we "do" history or chemistry or English literature. They care plenty when we expose some of them for the frauds they are.

It was no surprise to us, then, that many people who taught in universities didn't like what we had to say in our book. We thought our ideas would come under immediate attack, and we were not disappointed. What we didn't think would happen was that our right to ask uncomfortable questions about higher education would be challenged. We would not have believed that we would be attacked for "telling tales out of school." We would not have thought that the debate would have become highly personal or that others would try to marginalize us by accusing us of the foulest kind of thinking. We were wrong.

We did not mean *The Great Brain Robbery* to be a litmus test of Canadian academia's allegiance to the principle that free inquiry begins at home. But that's the way it turned out. And we're sorry to say that, for the most part, Canadian academia failed. We didn't want all those people out there who hated our little book to take it personally. We levelled not a single personal attack on anyone, though we did try to savage a number of organizations connected to the higher-education enterprise. But as soon as the book was published we learned how naive we were. We quickly became the "three blind mice" of Canadian academia, and much worse. We did take some solace when one student newspaper caricatured us as the Hitler, Mussolini, and Tojo of the professoriate. After all, we reasoned, someone *must* be studying history in order to make that connection!

The Great Brain Robbery took shape in the fall of 1983 when the three of us agreed that the institutions and the people who constituted higher education in Canada needed to account publicly for the poor job we believed they were doing with the taxpayer's money. Canada was then in the midst of the worst recession since the end of the Second World War, and many provincial governments had embarked on what we all thought then (before the Klein and Harris revolutions) were major budget cuts.

We were no more happy about budget cuts to universities than our colleagues. But unlike an apparent majority of our colleagues, we thought that most of the problems afflicting higher undergraduate education in Canada were not rooted in a shortage of funds. We did not believe that universities could be made better just by throwing money at them. We thought that systemic problems of attitude had hardened the arteries of so-called advanced education in all parts of Canada. We wrote *The Great Brain Robbery* to explain why we thought so, and to offer suggestions on how to fix the problems. It was aimed exclusively at problems we thought needed to be addressed in undergraduate education in Canada; we did not concern ourselves at all with graduate education.

The Great Brain Robbery advanced some outrageous notions for the mid-1980s:

- There were too many universities in Canada because governments had used new universities to bribe voters as once they had used new post offices.
- Tuition fees across Canada were far too low. These fee schedules had eroded university autonomy and given students a blasé attitude about wasting the heavy subsidies that taxpayers were pouring into every one of them.
- Entrance standards had virtually disappeared, and many students who were attending universities ought not to have been there.
- Tenure had become job security for incompetent academics whose continual failure to return good value for public-supported wages would otherwise have had them dismissed.
- Faculty unions cared more about wages for their members than the quality of education their members were delivering to the students.
- The all-round liberal arts education as a basis for all other learning had been replaced by trendy programs such as

"Canadian and other useless studies," as we dubbed one chapter.

- Students had too much freedom to decide what they needed to study. Curricula had become smorgasbords with too much light fare and not enough substantial learning.
- Grade inflation was undermining the value of a degree.
- University governance had become a swamp of incompetence and a morass of conflicting jurisdictions which blocked the emergence of virtually all creative thought.
- Too much democracy had crept into university governance. Students had too much say in determining strictly academic matters, as did university administrators.

Put simply, *The Great Brain Robbery* argued that disappearing provincial funds were *not* the major cause in the erosion of the quality of advanced education in Canada. The major problems were all connected to universities having become instruments of public policy rather than institutions of learning. Provincial governments wanted virtually anyone with a beating heart to gain entrance if he or she had a high school leaving certificate, because that was what the voters wanted.

We, in contrast, loudly proclaimed that everyone did *not* have a right to attend university, although everyone had a right to try to qualify to attend university — a very different thing. We were, and are, confirmed intellectual élitists in an age when very few of our fellow citizens, let alone our university colleagues, can make the basic distinction between what is a constitutionally guaranteed "right" and what must still be earned, qualified for, or achieved. We believed in equality of opportunity, not equality of outcome.

Because all three of us had been thinking similar thoughts on these matters for years, the book quickly took shape. The introduction outlined the problem as we saw it. The six substantive chapters were entitled: "The Funding Game," "Internal Democracy and the Road to Hell," "Studying in the Supermarket," "Tenure Is a Four-Letter Word," "The Perishing of Publishing," and "Canadian and Other Useless

Studies." In our conclusion, we argued that universities needed to put some good old-fashioned intellectual élitism back into the system — not élitism based on class, gender, or race, but élitism based on ability. We wanted the universities to take a good look at the systems then in use for recognizing and rewarding superior work by both faculty and students and to make sure those systems were working properly. We wanted less democracy, less faculty unionism, less student participation in academic decision making. We wanted to eliminate tenure, dismiss those of our colleagues who were incompetent, and give younger scholars fresh out of graduate schools a chance to be hired in place of the incompetent. We argued strongly for measures to stop grade inflation and to raise entrance standards. We sought an immediate increase in tuition fees and a generous expansion of bursary programs to help able students attend university, regardless of their ability to pay.

What we wanted most of all was for the men and women who led the advanced education enterprise in Canada in those days to begin to exercise their leadership to make the necessary changes. We had no doubt that if they did not, then governments would set the agenda for change in advanced education — and would do so with force and vigour. We were certainly right about that. With some notable exceptions, our leaders did not lead; government drove the change that occurred, and our leaders, for the most part, reacted. Today governments are getting the universities they want; we're not sure that students, faculty, or society are getting the universities they desire.

———

In 1997 Canada's publicly supported universities, employing some 27,000 full-time faculty and providing a place of study for a half-million students, are in deep trouble. The costs to maintain such a system are huge, and governments at all levels are reducing spending and forcing university administrations, with increasing desperation, to implement cutbacks and to offer early retirement packages to their older faculty. Tuition fees are rising for all students, most sharply in the professional schools. At the same time, we fear that standards are declining in the high schools and in the universities and that the quality of education is falling sharply, precisely when there are increasing numbers of competitors to traditional higher education. The virtual university is beginning to take shape, and the huge academic plants built with public funds all across the country may be on the cusp of obsolescence.

Do not fear for the faculty, however. Protected by tenure — which we view primarily as job security — they will survive, however unhappily. Faculty associations resist any effort to break away from tenure. They especially react against the idea of annual assessments and fixed-term renewable contracts which, we maintain, would protect those faculty who do their jobs well and allow the replacement of dullards with new blood from among the thousands of unemployed PhDs produced over the last decade by our expensive and publicly funded graduate schools.

We are deeply troubled by political correctness — the shrinking of the "traditional" university freedom to speak out about anything and the academic's freedom to research and write about any subject, however shocking it may be to delicate sensibilities. In the name of restricting speech that may offend someone, the universities, goaded by the provincial governments, are becoming frightened of ideas. The tradition of the university as a bastion of untrammelled thought is under attack as never before.

Nonetheless, the race to publish will continue, for publication is still the best way to get tenure. But increasingly what is published is, first, unreadable to the public and often even to other scholars, and, second, of little importance to anyone but the two or three specialists in the field. Journals and books, all dependent on subsidies and outrageously high prices, are flourishing like weeds in an untended garden. Surely it is time to look at the function of subsidies and to strive for fewer, but better and more readable, scholarly publications.

If this critique sounds less than hopeful, we still maintain that it is possible to get a good education in a Canadian university without taking a vow of poverty for the first ten years after graduation. With determination, investigation, and the ability to discriminate between showmanship and knowledge, students can make their way through the maze to emerge from university with a degree that means something and with the ability to read, think, and speak clearly and critically. Student debt remains a major difficulty, and faced with this, students and their parents should be demanding that old concept of value for money.

Canada needs good universities. It needs a system of higher education that can educate and train the ordinary citizens and the future leaders of this nation. It needs an educational system that can function efficiently, demonstrate that it has a proper concern for the quality of education offered, and encourage its professoriate to think the unthinkable, to challenge conventional wisdom, and to play a role in public debate. This book does not have all the answers, but we are certain that the existing system is not working as well as it should and that governments, administrations, and faculty associations, for their own reasons, are resistant to change. *Petrified Campus* is both a *cri de coeur* and a call for change.

Chapter 2

Bricks without Straw:
Financing Canada's Universities

IN 1995, WITHOUT ENTIRELY REALIZING IT, Canada's universities lost a political battle. It was a big battle, with drastic implications for the financial and institutional future of universities. Most professors, true to their ivory tower, did not realize that the battle had occurred, or that they and their students were destined to be big losers.

The government of Canada announced the conversion and reduction of existing federal transfers to the provinces, including a residual commitment to post-secondary education. These subsidies magically became the Canada Health and Social Transfer, or CHST. Public consultation was promised, and there was in fact some discussion, but as usual government had made up its mind. To deal with the greater evil, the deficit, Ottawa nerved itself to sacrifice its funding of universities. In the resulting proposals, not even a vestigial reference to federal support for universities remained.

The CHST was not an attention-grabber. Few Canadians are deeply interested in the elaborate protocol that keeps their federal state balanced between its federal and provincial wings. That money ("transfers") flows back and forth between the two principal levels of government would be news to most people, and of significantly less importance than the day's hockey or baseball scores.

If public attention is focused, it is on the "H" part of the acronym. Canadians do care about their health and their health funding. That is why the "H" is there — it was actually inserted at the insistence of the more socially minded members of the Liberal Cabinet. So why not education? The answer is unmistakable: education does not have the same political support as health. At a time when Canadian budgets are under attack, this is a serious business. Budgeting in the 1990s is a less-than-zero-sum game, and fiscal transfers are at the heart of the game.

University professors are not much better informed than their fellow citizens on the yawn-inducing subject of fiscal transfers. Perhaps most would know that, over the past forty-five years, Ottawa has set money aside for Canada's universities and has mailed it to the provinces to distribute ("transfers," again). They would probably not know how much of university budgets could be attributed to such activity. A few university administrators, the odd political scientist, and the occasional economist might notice, but for the majority of professors the news from Ottawa passed under their noses and over their heads.

Most of the time it would not matter. News is cheap, especially in the age of the information highway. Radio and television reporters thrive on daily alarms. The airwaves groan under the language of crisis, and there are so many examples — Quebec, Somalia, crime, taxes. Who had time for a little fiscal hanky-panky? And as for the Canadian Health and Social Transfer — a portentous name doubtless selected after exhaustive surveys and thousands of dollars in consultants' fees — why should that command more attention than the Established Program Financing it replaced? Public life is so stuffed with solemn nonsense that it is extremely difficult to sort out what is truly important from what merely sounds important.

But the Canadian Health and Social Transfer matters. It matters because it undermines the foundations of university finance as they have existed since the Second World War. It matters because universities have been nourished on federal subsidies and because their pattern of growth, their day-to-day existence, has been shaped by the expectation, the certainty, of money. Without subsidy, how will the universities cope?

They do not know. And thereby hangs our tale.

Like every tale it has a beginning, which for our purposes can be mercifully brief. The fundamental questions are "Why" and "How"?

Why did Canadians support universities, and how did they pay for them? As to why, universities were a cultural phenomenon imported from the Old World with the colonists. Embedded in society and society's expectations, they sprang up almost as soon as Europeans set foot in North America — Harvard in 1636, and a host of colleges thereafter. New France had a seminary for priestly education before the British Conquest in 1760, and it eventually developed into Laval University; the English-language colleges followed — McGill, Dalhousie, Toronto, and all the rest.

Universities began small and, through the nineteenth century and into the twentieth, stayed small. They could be financed by government or by religious sects, with an assist from student fees, because their cost was small. Public-spirited citizens, who were sometimes alumni, made donations and sometimes set up endowments. On one spectacular occasion the treasurer of the University of Manitoba vanished with most of that university's money, but for the most part the universities eked along, educated their undergraduates, and paid their faculty according to the cycles of the economy. The faculty read books, wrote articles, and engaged in the miniature politics of the university. They were not expected to do much else.

By the end of the nineteenth century, research was creeping in and, with it, professionalization. Research might have value beyond the university — better strains of wheat, for example, or a better way of milling ore would make Canada more prosperous and favour the balance of payments. These were national concerns, or so it could plausibly be argued. Through agriculture and then technology, Ottawa began to spend money on educating people, for you could not have proper research without at least some educational foundation — and that meant university education.

This trend was happening in other countries, too. The ones Canadians knew about — the United States, Great Britain, the countries of Western Europe — had alternatives Canadians did not have: large corporations able to finance their own research; charitable foundations with the ability to sponsor even more; and universities with ancient and plentiful endowments. Canada, alas, was recent, and its big fortunes were few and of recent date. University endowments suffered by comparison with those in the United States. Similarly, Canada had few charitable foundations. The National Research Council in Ottawa, founded in 1916, dispensed grants and conducted its own research — but on a shoestring. It was a beginning and a precedent, but until the Second World War not much more.

Research was conducted in other fields too, especially in history and the social sciences, which were enlisted by governments in the 1920s and 1930s to examine and predict Canada's social, economic, and political situation. It was high time, because during the 1930s Canada was afflicted by an economic depression of unprecedented severity; academics were called on to explain why and to suggest ways of getting out of a hole that private enterprise seemed to have dug. By the time of the Second World War, Canadian academics had grouped themselves into professional associations and were seeking to establish professional standards.

The experience of war underlined the usefulness of research. The 1939–45 war was a technologists' delight, a war fought and won by machinery and therefore by scientists and engineers. It was also a theorist's delight, as economists experimented with Swedish tax systems and Keynesian spending, and speculated about cycles of boom and bust. Political scientists and historians worked on the development and expansion of democracy, while humanists tried to define what a good society should know and what it should learn.

Not everybody was convinced. At the height of the war, economist Cyril James, the principal of McGill University, proposed shutting down the humanities departments at Canada's universities so they could concentrate on war-winning science. It was an idea that did not receive the attention, or derision, it deserved, but it was in any case short lived. Canadian universities did not cost enough for even the maddest politician to believe that much money would be saved by putting Latin professors to work in some more productive occupation — knitting socks, or pounding steel in a tank factory. James, however, kept his job and went on to glory as the reputed father of Canada's social welfare system — an exaggerated claim that attentive historians have not yet dispelled.

To make a long story short, universities ended the war firmly established as citadels of practical activity: science, of course, which helped to produce the much-admired atomic bomb; engineering, which dug tunnels under Gibraltar to keep the Germans at bay; economics, which produced Canada's centralized tax system and damped down inflation; and the humanities, which symbolized and justified democracy's struggle against tyranny, first Nazi and then communist.

Better still, universities helped to solve Canada's most immediate postwar problem: what to do with a million veterans of the wartime armed forces. Infused with federal cash, Canada's universities rose to the challenge and churned out thousands of service people, who then populated the nation's classrooms as teachers for the baby boom generation that was coming on. The boomers would have to be especially well educated, good citizens as well as good technicians and scientists, because the challenge from tyranny had not died with Adolf Hitler in 1945. The 1940s and 1950s confronted communism in the Cold War. As in the previous hot war, universities were part of the response, both because they improved the West's external defences, the kind represented by the growing nuclear stockpile, and because they shored up society's internal defences — as an instrument for social progress through a highly educated and intelligent population.

Politics and university economics were firmly linked. Under the circumstances, it was unpatriotic to question the utility of universities — it was self-evident. Across the border in the United States the federal government gave out billions in grants and subsidies to American institutions. A whole generation of PhDs was educated under the provisions of a statute called the National Defense Education Act. Students of seventeenth-century witchcraft, philosophers pursuing justice, aficionados of microbiology all benefited, and the result was a quantum leap in learning in the United States.

The United States is and has been the strongest external influence on Canada. What happens in the United States will sooner or later find an echo in Canada. In the 1940s and 1950s Canadians hardly needed encouragement. Their own experience of war, the benefits derived from Canada's existing university-educated population, and the highly successful conversion of the war veterans into tweedy and blue-stockinged BAs, MAs, and PhDs all confirmed the wisdom of the American policy of rewarding learning.

It was also a time for nationalism and federal initiatives. Both the 1930s Depression and the Second World War were nationalizing experiences as far as Canada was concerned. These were gigantic events to which Canada could not effectively respond except on a national basis. Confronted with war across the world, Canada's provincial governments — even Quebec's — looked puny and inconsequential. Though universities were provincial in their origins and their basic finance, their inhabitants, professors and students, became national if not international in their orientation.

In postwar Canada, everywhere but Quebec, this broader perspective did not really matter. Even the Social Credit government of Alberta, arguably Canada's most peculiar, did not significantly object to a Cold War educational climate that stressed large (i.e., non-provincial) responses to great international problems. It is a fair bet that ever since the Second World War the majority of Canadian faculty have voted Liberal (minorities would vote NDP or Conservative) on the federal and frequently the provincial scene, reflecting an attachment to Canada's national — some would say natural — governing party. This phenomenon applies no matter where you are in Canada, and holds true even in elections when the Liberals have been heavily chastised by the Canadian electorate.

The Liberals were in power in Canada during that war and after. That fact, as much as any ideology, helped determine the attachment of Canada's professoriate to the Governing Party. And it arose in the question of federal finance for universities.

There are two levels in interpreting what happened next. The first is the temporary, expedient, political level, the level of the Cold War. In the 1950s, Canadians were very frightened of what would happen if the West lost the Cold War. The Korean War broke out in 1950 and Canada sent troops. In 1951, Canada sent troops back to Europe. That same year, the Canadian government announced that, in the interests of national defence, it would send money to universities. Some of the officials who devised this policy were themselves ex-professors, and some of the Cabinet ministers who approved it were also ex-professors — the prime minister, the minister of finance, the minister of national defence, the minister of external affairs, among others. A former university president was minister of labour. It was a friendly audience.

These friendly officials also granted money to universities because they thought it was a Good Thing. This is the second level of explanation for the subsidies. Some Canadians in the years after the Second World War worried about the Americanization of their country. Indeed, Canadians in every generation worry about this topic: they did in the 1800s, in the 1900s, and in the 1990s. The 1950s were no different. Feeding Canadian culture would help prevent the Americanization of Canada *and* assist the standard-bearers of culture generally — the universities.

The friendly audience could get away with financing universities *not* because most Canadians agreed it was a good idea to hand over money to Canada's remote ivory towers but because of two practical reasons. First, the country was prosperous and the money could be spared; and, second, universities were thought to contribute directly to society's welfare and survival. They fostered science and industry, developed actual and psychological weapons, and helped to win the Cold War.

Canada's provinces, for the most part, were not displeased. Federal largesse got them off the hook, as it did with the construction of the Trans-Canada Highway at the same time. Money Ottawa donated for perceptibly improved services, universities, and highways did not have to be raised by provinces in taxes or paid by university students in increased fees. Ontario and Alberta were spared sales taxes through the 1950s, and their citizens travelled on good federally funded roads while their children attended federally funded universities at rates that in constant dollars were actually declining. Best of all from the politicians' point of view, their tax-paring provincial governments were regularly re-elected.

At the same time, the federal government entered the research game in a big way. A windfall from estate taxes allowed the government to establish the Canada Council to dispense grants to the arts and social sciences — another coup for culture. Forgotten in the glow of appreciation was the backhanded way the new granting agency was financed, another sign of the marginal nature of research in Canada.

With finances in better shape than ever before, Canadian universities were in a position to meet the arrival of the baby boom in the mid-1960s. Capital grants built new buildings, research funds financed new learning, and Canada Council scholarships trained new professors. And just in time. Canada's student population jumped from 113,729 in 1960 to 309,469 in 1970. Between 1960 and 1966, the number of teachers in Canadian universities grew from 9200 to 15,900. Between 1966 and 1971, the total grew again, to 24,733.

Canadian faculty, who had previously relied on American fellowships or capriciously granted sabbatical leaves, had arrived in the promised land. They knew what the promised land was by glancing across the border, and often put their knowledge to work by moving there. The federal government was not oblivious to what it was doing: there was a strong nationalistic component to its approach to university finance and to research grants. As a result, Canadian faculty members were encouraged to stay in Canada, and Canadians abroad were enticed to return.

As in the 1950s, the finance boom of the 1960s rode on another, larger trend. Canadians were completing a welfare state in the 1960s, and universities for all were part of the package.[1] Relying on the last

---

1. Canadians like to think that their welfare state helps define them as a country. "Traditionally," it is said, Canadians have a stronger social safety net to protect them than do the Americans. "Tradition" is a wonderful word, beloved of politicians and other commentators. It can mean almost anything while conveying powerful feelings of authenticity. In this case, it means "about thirty years."

stages of the postwar boom, Canadians in the 1960s voted themselves an expanded social safety net of pensions and medicare. Because they had previously provided themselves with an unprecedented number of children, they also plumped for public education of all kinds, including universities. Universities in the 1960s tripled in size, responding to a generous federal scheme of grants. The federal government gave directly to universities, and it lent to students to go to universities. Provinces, under the constitution the masters of education, scrambled to keep up with a record number of students whose voter-parents wanted them to have a university education. And so more universities were founded — Simon Fraser, Lethbridge, Regina, York, Trent, Sherbrooke — sometimes on the ruins of more lowly foundations, sometimes not.

Economic prosperity plus a population surge created a unique situation for universities. A more prosperous population believed that Canada could afford more in the way of education than ever before. Canada had always lagged behind the United States — Canadians' only international standard of comparison — in education as in other fields. Now Canadians could catch up. As they did: for the first time in history, Canadians' standard of living caught up with that of their rich American cousins.

In the mid-1960s universities derived their income from four sources: endowments (3.7% in 1962); tuition (27%); government grants, federal and provincial (58%), with the balance made up by "miscellaneous." The resulting mix, the fact that the practitioners of higher learning could call on two paymasters, was pleasing to universities. Money from several sources was preferable to single-source funding — government aid administered by provinces alone. The provincial governments of the 1950s and 1960s were for the most part generous to universities, and at the same time relieved that the federal government through its subsidies was assuming a large part of their financial burdens. These burdens grew during the 1960s, as more universities opened and expanded to take care of the baby boom children. There was, or appeared to be, more money for all — and so a hundred academic flowers bloomed, seeded, and proliferated.

It isn't hard for an institution — any institution, whether it's a private corporation, a government department, or a university — to adjust to growth. "Just say yes" might as well be the motto. Not enough buildings? Build another! Professors not quite up to snuff? Why bother with a messy and uncomfortable decision to fire anybody? Hire more! Hard decisions on curriculum? Why reassign people when it's easy to add another body to the budget! Litigious students? Hire more staff, print more forms, create more committees! More was beautiful, in a time of plenty.

The "more" method of governance perfectly suited the "me" generation. Spending more money created an illusion of flexibility and, better still, liberalism. In fact, however, universities were building in rigidity. Abandoning internal controls — the ability or the desire to say no — stored up trouble. Repeatedly saying yes created more than expectations for the future: it helped form a conviction that more of everything — money, students, professors — would solve whatever problems ailed the university, or society in general. A large segment of the professoriate came to believe that universities were a model in which society's problems would be solved; unfortunately, universities tend to be a mirror in which most of society's problems are reflected.

More professors, more buildings, more students, and more costs resulted in more taxes, more spending, and, ultimately, more deficits. Canadian tax rates were broadly comparable to American in 1960; that was no longer the case by 1970, and even less true by 1980. The political burden for the federal government grew too: the provinces were becoming quarrelsome and assertive. They demanded more control over fields that constitutionally were theirs. The Liberal government in Ottawa had problems with the Liberal government in Quebec, which was asserting an autonomist agenda. In 1966 the political balance shifted.

Anxious to extricate itself from open-ended commitments to the universities, and bowing in the direction of the then-fashionable doctrine of "cooperative federalism," the federal government announced that in future it would cooperate with the provinces in a 50/50 shared-cost program in which one federal dollar must be equalled by one provincial dollar. There was still control and accountability under this system. Then, in 1977, the federal government went one step beyond. Creating something called Established Programs Financing, the federal government announced that it was now time to trust the provinces to administer the well-established programs previously watched over by Ottawa.[2]

Not everybody was convinced. There were warnings, but as usual when governments have other objects in mind, it was easy to override facts and logic. Abandoning shared cost and operating instead on the principle of trust was rash, and inevitably it reaped the harvest of its folly. The economy was not doing as well as it had done in the 1960s, and in the 1970s there were other priorities for government. Education became a lower priority. As a recent study put it, with reference to Ontario, "the share of Government spending allocated to universities has declined consistently from year to year," meaning, in 1997, for twenty years. Other provinces did better, but not much. By comparison, the American states' appropriations for their public universities fell, rose, fell again, and rose again, following the convolutions of the economy. Where they ended up, however, is significantly above the standing of Canadian universities.[3]

As the rate of growth slowed in the Canadian economy in the 1970s, unemployment rose and inflation became a serious problem. There were real crises at home and abroad — Quebec, for example, and a tenfold increase in the price of oil. Crisis times seemed to demand emergency measures, but while the crises passed, the measures stayed. Governments of the 1970s treated the symptoms of problems rather

2. The money transferred to the provinces, beginning in 1967–68, was significantly greater than earlier forms of federal aid, approaching $1 billion in 1972–73. The impact of all this aid, plus increased finance from the provinces, boosted the total government proportion of university revenues to 76 percent in 1970–71.

3. Council of Ontario Universities, *The Financial Position of Universities in Ontario, 1995*, 7, 12, 15–16.

than the problems themselves. Less acute problems were for the most part frozen, then shelved. Universities were such a problem.

Growth shuddered to a halt on campuses across the land. Construction slowed, along with faculty hirings. But most faculty were young, recently hired, and university buildings were young, too. There was no immediate reason to worry. University enrolment, which was expected to rise steadily through the decade, instead fluctuated up and down. So did university finance, typically based on student numbers. Faculty salaries were eroded by inflation, reducing the gains of the 1960s. Yet even this cloud had a silver lining — professors had tenure, and tenure protected jobs. The link between declining real incomes and permanent employment was real; and, typically, it was not perceived. Tenure became a component in university finance, and it certainly played a role in keeping the aging and increasingly cash-strapped employees docile if not happy.

There was another ominous cloud on the horizon. The baby boom had ended. Birth rates fell, and in the 1970s first elementary and then secondary schools were beginning to empty. The schools responded by redistributing rather than reducing their resources, and funding for primary and secondary education continued to rise. Demographers predicted and governments concluded that the same enrolment decline would happen to universities. Under the circumstances, it was prudent to switch universities' diet from "growth" to "maintenance."

University finance was helped by one unexpected windfall. Students, lacking opportunity in the stagnant job climate of the 1970s, stayed in school. Adolescence was prolonged, and as professors sprouted grey hairs, so did their students. And why not? University funding was based in part on enrolment. More scholars, more dollars. More bodies in individual classrooms too, and more demands on individual professors, but with some grumbling the professors shouldered the burdens.

Throughout the 1970s, the federal government continued to give money to the provinces for higher education, but with fewer and fewer strings attached. Federal funding was nevertheless very important. In

1979–80, for example, for "provincial" funding of $4.2 billion for universities there was a federal contribution of $2.8 billion.[4] As these figures suggest, some provinces spent less on higher education than they received from the federal government for that purpose. Highways were paved and hospitals opened. University administrators who protested were told, bluntly, to pipe down. Compared with other segments of the population, universities had nothing to complain about — an assertion that was broadly true. The money did not flow as abundantly, but governments did not interfere with universities' ability to run their own affairs. And universities, like everybody else, postponed their problems and their solutions. Like society in general, Canada's universities passed through the 1970s forgetting nothing and learning nothing.

Government support continued to be the dominant factor in university finance. In 1979–80, fees "and other sources" represented 16 percent of university revenue, and fees alone were estimated to account for no more than 12.5 percent of the total. Low fees had become a potent political toy in the provincial governments' shop-window, and as a result university education in Canada during the 1970s and early 1980s was a bonanza for students. Fees did not stay abreast of inflation, but increased government funding covered the resulting gap.

Then Canada entered the economic roller-coaster of the 1980s. There was a severe recession in 1981–82, the first since 1954. The economy recovered in 1983, but unemployment in the rest of the decade was higher than it had been in the 1970s, and higher again than in the 1960s. The "temporary" cutbacks in universities in the 1970s became the permanent austerity of the 1980s. Hirings again were affected, with a particular impact on young women, who were entering the would-be professoriate in sizeable numbers for the first time. Full-time female

---

4. A bizarre federal publication, *Profile of Post-Secondary Education in Canada, 1993* (Ottawa 1994) credits "provincial governments" with 60 percent of university support in 1971–72 and 67 percent in 1981–82 (29).

professors increased from 4781 in 1977–78 to 6381 in 1987–88, out of a total professoriate of about 35,000, but this was at a time when women had become a majority of university students. As another consequence, senior professors (mostly male, mostly born before 1945) increased in proportion to junior ones. Senior employees earn more money than junior ones practically everywhere: even by just standing still and hiring nobody, universities' salary costs were rising.

The 1980s were an extravagant but uncertain interlude in Canadian public finance. Taxes rose, but so did government deficits. The federal government attempted to save money by capping transfers to the wealthier provinces, while continuing to shovel money in the direction of volatile Quebec and the Atlantic provinces. Funds for universities did increase, but not enough to match another jump in enrolment from 382,617 in 1980 to 532,132 in 1990. Needless to say, the provinces did not rush to make up the vanished funding. Computed on a per-student basis, university grants declined steadily from 1977–78 on. Though there was more money, it was much more thinly spread.

That was the picture as the recession of 1990–91 manifested itself. That recession was on the whole less severe than the downturn of 1981, but its aftermath was enduring. Indeed, in some respects, Canada has still not surmounted the after-effects of this recession. Canadian unemployment climbed to European levels and stayed there.[5] Anaemic economic recovery, combined with high and continuing unemployment and a fall in real terms of individual after-tax income, all mean fewer resources for government. As for the public, a Revolution of Declining Expectations set in.

There was not even the Cold War to console our scholars. In the 1950s, universities were part of the Western world's response to communist tyranny. By mobilizing minds, by exploiting knowledge and

---

5. Unemployment rose from 7.5 percent in 1989 to 11.3 percent in 1992. Though it has dipped slightly since then, it remains high — roughly 10 percent in early 1997.

science, the theory went, we would eventually prevail over communism.[6] But knowledge and science did not survive the Cold War unscathed. Cold Warriors grew older, popular enthusiasm flagged, and the link between science, knowledge, universities, and money, once taut and pulsing with cash, sagged. The end of the Cold War in 1989 removed the last remnant of the expensive ideological garments that once clothed Canada's higher education.

All was not entirely lost, however. Puzzling their way around the stagnation, inflation, and rising unemployment of the 1970s and 1980s, economists observed that there was a correlation between more education and less unemployment. For society, education, knowledge, and research remained the route to more prosperity — even in Canada. But, in one of its frequent contradictions, society approved of and wanted research, but was unwilling to pay for it. In 1991–92, as Canada's federal election approached, any one of the major American research schools — Stanford, University of Washington, Michigan, Johns Hopkins — received more research funding than all the universities in Ontario combined.[7]

Canada's governments — federal and provincial, Conservative, Liberal, and NDP — all paid tribute to research and, with it, education. The Liberal Party, in its collection of election promises for 1993, the Red Book, promised that it would not only care for research and culture but would foster them. Once elected, however, the Liberal government found that the Red Book was not a reliable guide.

For one thing, there was the federal deficit. It worried the press, it preoccupied public opinion, and it panicked investors. To deal with increasingly negative perceptions of Canada and its public finances, the Liberals discreetly remaindered their Red Book and placed themselves in a deficit-fighting mode. In the political and economic climate of 1993–94, something had to give. The federal Liberals were not

---

6. As we did. All over the world, communism collapsed at the end of the 1980s.
7. Council of Ontario Universities, Financial Position, 1995, 23.

necessarily prejudiced against either research or universities, but they had a Problem.

———

"The capacities of our federal-provincial governments to finance us is declining," according to David Johnston, whose gloom overwhelmed his syntax on this occasion; but he should have known, since he was, after all, ex-principal of McGill. "It [sic] will continue to do so at least into the next millennium." Worse, "the wealth generating capacity of Canada has declined in relative terms by over 20% in the past two decades. Public expenditures, including university operating grants and research and capital support, are beyond the capacity of the state to pay. We shall not be spared."[8] A short time later, another ex-principal, David Smith of Queen's University, chimed in with a jeremiad of his own. In September 1996 Smith told a reporter that "the public source of funding for the system that we built isn't there."[9]

Well, not exactly *not there*. As we all know, in a good cause a little exaggeration never hurt anyone. By *not there* we mean *less available*. The Liberal government in Ottawa may be many things, and it has been called most of them. But it is not quite the heavy in a remake of Godzilla versus Bambi, and the universities are not precisely Bambi — happy, lucky, and carefree. They are, rather, closer to the Seven Dwarfs — happy, hapless, and stupid. Let us take these three qualities one by one.

Happy. Canada has eighty-eight universities, including theological schools and other religious colleges, spread from coast to coast. They grant degrees of all kinds, from BAs to PhDs, and they cherish visions, most of them, of being the Harvard of the North or the East, or

8. David L. Johnston, *Research at Canadian Universities and the Knowledge-Based Society, 1995 Killam Lecture*, published by the Killam Trustees 13.

9. Toronto *Globe and Mail*, 4 September 1996.

wherever. We should allow a variation for francophone institutions, which aspire to the Sorbonne or one of the *grandes écoles*. These visions were seeded by the prosperity of the 1960s and frozen by the academic policies of the 1970s and 1980s. The greatest wish of Canada's universities is to survive; next in line, barely, is that they should keep on doing more or less what they do at present. If the money can be found, this is one definition of happiness.

Hapless. Hapless is defined as unlucky, accident-prone. Universities have been sand-bagged by their belief that government finance is stable, reliable, and desirable. Desirable it surely is, but experience shows that it is subject to many variables — economic, constitutional, and political. It is not, and has not been, stable or reliable. But universities have remained confused by their misinterpretation of the bargain they struck back in the 1950s. Universities believed and still believe that the government was moved by a desire to enhance culture. They also believe that because they spoke with one voice when the going was good and the money flowing, this is an indicator of a common interest. Unfortunately, Canada's universities have many interests, and they are not the same. As a result, universities spend a great deal of time and effort on self-contradiction, when their energies might better be spent on self-promotion.

As for government, the case is simpler. The government believed that it was fighting the Cold War by mobilizing yet another resource — intellectuals. The Cold War is over, and nothing, as far as government is concerned, has taken its place.

Stupid. Universities pretend to be united, focused on a common goal, but in fact they are not. Not only are Canadian universities divided by size, location, ambition, and function but their individual component parts are, to put it gently, incoherent. This means that each university speaks with at least three voices — administration, faculty, and students.

Administrations are bound to pretend that they speak for all, and we believe that they actually try to take all their diverse interests into account. Unfortunately, this attempt to create unity from diversity means that administrations must use concealment as their operating tool, which sows distrust among their clients — faculty and students. These respond by pursuing their own goals, thereby undermining what the administration is trying, ineptly, to do. The result is to make universities a bad bargaining partner for government, because government can never, will never, know just what is coming next.

Demanding, rigid, and incoherent at the same time, Canada's universities faced a Liberal government in Ottawa that, as of the fall of 1993, did not know its own mind, and, despite the Red Book, was undecided what to do with its mandate and how to do it. This lack of firm conviction made the Liberals easy prey for the first crisis to come by — the Canadian budgetary crisis and the Quebec election of September 1994. The politics of Quebec, where the Liberal government under Daniel Johnson was going down to defeat at the hands of the separatists, dictated that the federal government tread carefully where provincial jurisdiction was concerned, and post-secondary education was definitely provincial. The effect was to postpone Liberal initiatives in social policy generally, and in post-secondary education in particular, through the summer of 1994. It didn't stop there, because after the Quebec Liberals were defeated and a referendum on Quebec independence became inevitable, any possible federal incursions into provincial jurisdiction were carefully scrutinized and, if at all possible, put on ice. That did not quite happen to the federal government's post-secondary education finance proposals, when they emerged in October 1994, but it affected the climate in which they would be considered.

By that time the magnitude of Canada's deficit had begun to sink in where it really counted, in the mind of the wily and increasingly powerful minister of finance, Paul Martin. Several times in 1994, one minister recalled, the country came "close to the wall" — that is, unable to borrow the money to pay Canada's current bills. The minister of finance made sure his colleagues knew about the problem. As he intended, they were impressed.

Probably rightly, the government decided it must lower Canada's high deficits. The main instrument was the conversion and reduction of existing federal transfers to the provinces — the Established Programs Financing, which still retained a residual, if nominal, commitment to post-secondary education.[10] These subsidies would magically become the Canada Health and Social Transfer, or CHST.

It was not the best acronym from the universities' point of view. Much better, more pronounceable, more inclusive, would have been CHEST — Canadian Health, *Education*, and Social Transfer. But it didn't happen.

Why not? The story begins some time before the CHST was devised or conceived — shortly after the Liberals took office in 1993. Those close to the action divided the federal Cabinet into three or four groups when it came to the "university question." There were those who saw the universities as industrial annexes, churning out practical research for Canada's factories. There were visionaries who were mesmerized by the arrival of the great information highway and who speculated whether universities of the old-fashioned kind were really necessary. There were ministers who themselves had passed through university and had not liked the experience — who saw Canada's universities as engines of intellectual fraud and personal incompetence. And there were those, a minority, who thought that the universities were essential and should, somehow, be sustained. These included the responsible minister, Lloyd Axworthy, himself a PhD from Princeton, a 1960s radical with a residual regard for universities and their ways.

Axworthy had a number of problems. The biggest problem was that he was not the only minister with a stake in higher education. His particular province was students — human resources. But research fitted elsewhere, in the domain of John Manley, the industry minister, while science was confided to a junior minister, Jon Gerrard. Divided

---

10. Federal transfers to the provinces are of two kinds. First, there is cash, and second, there are "tax points." Cash is cash, but tax points are something else. Theoretically, the federal government "vacates" x percent of a tax field, which the provinces then "occupy." The taxes "forgone" by Ottawa are then toted up and applied to the transfer total. The provinces increasingly view this portion of federal transfers as funny money.

jurisdiction placed a premium on cooperation among the three ministers, and especially on developing a common timetable. Axworthy studied students while Manley studied research, but they studied them at
different speeds. And when Axworthy was ready, Manley was not.

What they had in common was the $2 billion or so in federal fund-
ing supposedly directed at universities under the Established Programs
Financing. According to the formula devised in 1977, money flowed
from Ottawa, supposedly for post-secondary education. But it was sent
off on an honours system, and there were ample reasons to believe that
the provinces did not use it all for universities. Axworthy proposed to
replace this creaky and increasingly farcical system with a program of
student loans — $2 billion per annum, of which, experience showed,
about $1.5 billion could actually be recovered, for a total putative cost to
the treasury of $500 million a year.

This apparent cost could be presented as a massive saving to an
economy-minded Cabinet. This Axworthy and Gerrard, his fellow-
Manitoban, did. But other ministers were nervous. Did the students
like the proposal?

Evidently not. Axworthy made a primary political error in devising
and then presenting his reforms. He linked his student loan program to
rising university fees. Axworthy was taking away university funding
from provinces with one hand and creating obligations for students
with the other. Provinces would pass on the shortfall in federal funding
to universities, and universities would pass it on to students in the form
of higher tuition fees. Students would borrow from Axworthy's fund
and go more deeply into debt. This was not an attractive proposition to
most student leaders and, not surprisingly, Axworthy's reforms became
unpopular on campuses virtually overnight. At the same time, notions
about tuition fee rates did not go down well with the provinces, especially Quebec, always jealous of federal interference.

Axworthy's preliminary proposals, embodied in a draft green
paper (which in government jargon is something short of a policy paper
to which the Cabinet as a whole is committed), originally included a
research component. The research component did not survive Cabinet

scrutiny: ministers wanted research to be managed by Manley, and Manley was not ready. Only the student funding proposal went forward, and it was already mortally wounded.

To prevail in Cabinet, Axworthy and his allies needed something like a united front from Canada's university community — professors, students, administrators, and boards of governors. They did not get it. Canada's universities, faced with a threat to "their" (well, the provinces') transfer payments, did what imperilled institutions often do — they fought among themselves. The larger universities, Canada's "Big Ten," from UBC to Laval, urged the case for "excellence." They were research institutions, the ones with research capacity, and they should be funded first. What was left over could be assigned to the lesser universities, who must fend for themselves.

The lesser schools did not like the tune of this song. They replied that they were teaching institutions, they produced the university-educated graduates essential to Canada's future, and in any case their institutions were economic engines in their communities. They mobilized their resources, and they had many local members of parliament.

The students and professors contributed too. The professors sang mostly from the same songbook, devised by their national union, or kept quiet. More professors, naturally, were the solution, and more money — not a refrain that was especially welcome or appropriate. The students, a livelier bunch, fought among themselves over what kind of help they should get. Some decided it would be clever to picket Lloyd Axworthy's home one evening. While the minister dined inside, the students (or, possibly, pseudo-students) raved outside. As they doubtless intended, Axworthy took note. Unfortunately for their cause, it was not a favourable notice. Equally unfortunately, others noticed too. The minister's friends in the universities, observed the deputy minister of finance, "were kicking the shit out of him."[11]

---

11. Quoted in Edward Greenspan and Anthony Wilson-Smith, *Double Vision: The Inside Story of the Liberals in Power* (Toronto 1996), 229.

Unable to mobilize a credible united front from a disunited and leaderless university community, university advocates in the government lunged for modifications or exemptions in the federal cuts as they affected universities. There they ran into a roadblock. The Cabinet agreed there had to be cuts. For the cuts to be acceptable, they had to be "fair" — that is, applied to everyone. One exemption would lead to another and the result would be, first, chaos, and next, the failure of the cuts exercise. The universities were unable to mount a plausible lobby. Instead, they did a pretty good job of demonstrating that the politicians did not have to be afraid of them. Left to their own devices, the universities would fight among themselves.

————————

Defeat on the federal front left universities confronting the provinces in their search for money. The provinces had already let it be known, in a hundred subtle ways, that they were no longer prepared to foot the whole bill for universities. This decision applied no matter what the political complexion of the province, and, after a certain lag, it even leaped Canada's linguistic barrier between Quebec and the rest of the country.

The clearest sign of changing times was a decrease in the proportion of university costs that governments were willing to finance. Government subsidy as a percentage of university budgets fell from 80 percent in 1984 to 74 percent in 1994. Tuition rose as a percentage of income from 16 to 23.1 percent in the same decade.[12] As a consequence, while Canadian support for universities remains high, government support for universities is less high.

In Ontario, Bob Rae's NDP government let it be known that fees could rise — by 10 percent. The NDP, of course, was facing decimation at the polls, but the fact that Canada's most left-wing government could

———————————

12. *Globe and Mail*, 9 October 1995.

actually contemplate what by its standards was a socially regressive act was a measure of its financial distress. But when Rae's government was defeated, the incoming Harris Conservatives raised the 10 percent fee increase to 20 percent.

Universities did not have to implement the increase: they could keep fees low if they wished and hope to attract more students that way. Or they could contemplate the future and ask themselves whether 20 percent was really going to be the end of the game. If there was little public outcry, the Ontario government, and other governments, would surely cut more in the future. What if the real solution was 30 percent, 40 percent, 50 percent?

In the meantime, universities took what they could get. Even student-challenged Carleton, which confronts a drastic decline in enrolment, felt it had to charge the full 20 percent increase. The University of Toronto and the University of Western Ontario, which operate Ontario's only dental schools, asked for and got permission to raise fees to $8000 a year — double the previous rate. These were American levels of tuition — the same as at some American state universities. Did this mean that Canada should follow, one more time, an American model for universities? Could Canada follow such a model?

Out-of-border experiences are typically Canadian, since for Canadians their country exists in symbiosis with its admired (and hated and feared) larger twin. American practice is not irrelevant to Canadians, as a long history of Canadian imitation of the United States testifies.

There is an equally long history of repudiation, also based on the American example: conscious lack of imitation is the sincerest form of flattery. Mostly, however, there is imitation pure and simple. The creation of Canada's state-funded universities in the first place had much to do with what had happened over the border. The expansion of the Canadian university system in the 1960s directly mimicked an earlier American educational explosion. But unlike the United States, Canada did not develop a variety of university types; in particular, it did not develop universities with large endowments like Stanford, Harvard, or

Princeton. For a brief moment in the 1960s, there might have been the hope that by mobilizing public resources — subsidies derived from taxes — Canada's universities would eventually rival those in the United States; but the dispersal of Canadian resources among regions and provinces, along with the country's parochial politics, made that not merely an unlikely but an impossible dream. The dream coincided with a spasm of anti-Americanism, which tinged Canadian politics, at least in English Canada, from the 1950s into the 1980s.

In the conservative climate of the later 1980s and 1990s, however, the United States was officially rehabilitated from its periodic role of Canadian demon and restored to a position of respect, a model worthy of imitation. The Americans had low taxes (and, in the 1980s, large deficits); Canadians must imitate them. The Americans had a vigorous form of free enterprise; Canada too must set its businessmen free — unless they needed subsidy, of course. American universities charged higher tuition than their Canadian counterparts: Could Canada not do the same?

There was a real issue behind these discussions. Some Canadians, many Canadians in fact, were spending more on their children's university training. Those who could afford it sometimes spent a lot more. Canadians were leaving Canada to go to the United States for their university education at roughly three to five times the cost than to stay at home — for a non-resident student not on scholarship. In 1993–94, the last year for which statistics are available, there were 22,600 Canadian students of all kinds in the United States. And, of course, many more young Canadians leave home to study somewhere else, out of city or out of province, reminding us that university is a rite of passage as well as a school of advanced cramming. And some of those who do not leave take another path of departure, by studying at a distance, in the various forms of "Distance Ed."

From the perspective of funding and money, the differences between Canadian universities and their American cousins are striking. American private universities receive *twice* the funding, per student, that universities in Canada's richest province, Ontario, do.

According to data from the late 1980s, American private universities had roughly five times the endowment income *per student* that Ontario universities had. Income from "gifts" was also larger — about three times. For those who talk glibly about imitating the American experience in all its forms, of creating a Harvard of the North, these are instructive figures.

A more relevant comparison can be made than to Harvard, Yale, Princeton, all old, richly endowed, private universities. Canadian universities were not, after all, founded to be like the Ivy League. Rather, they were related, if distantly, to the American state schools — Ohio, Michigan, Illinois, Colorado. Here, a comparison brings out startling points of resemblance. American state schools, for example, have endowment income that on a per-student basis is less than that of Ontario universities. They make more money from tuition and other fees, 80 percent more in 1988–89. American public university fees may serve as a benchmark for what may be achievable and politically possible, in the short run, for Canadian public universities.

There are, however, some less malleable differences. American public universities still get one-third more income, per student, than their Canadian counterparts. The larger part of the difference between Canadian and American state schools lies in higher state appropriations for comparable universities and in research funding from the U.S. federal government — much higher than in Canada. It is double the Canadian amount for public universities, and over five times higher, per student, for private universities.

This last fact should serve to remind us that there is almost no such thing, even in the free-enterprise United States, as a totally private university, "free" from public support of all kinds. Even Harvard depends heavily on research contracts, mostly public, to support its lifestyle and that of its faculty members. American research and development, R&D, relies massively on universities, their faculty and facilities. It is very unlikely that this practice will be seriously altered.

Nor are American universities free from public regulation and direction. In Ohio, whose population is about the same size as neighbouring

Ontario's, the state government decided it was time to cut costs. It intervened to tell its public universities what they could teach and where, based on an assessment of each school's strengths and weaknesses. Instead of allowing every university to be a full-service institution, Ohio decided that one of a kind within its state boundaries was surely enough. The universities, or rather their faculties, howled their protest, but failed to prevail.

Such detailed micro-management is expensive and usually controversial, as Ohio's experience shows. There are other, blunter instruments to hand. We noted above that reductions in government support for universities have created, in theory, more room for universities to set their own prices and to manage their own policies. The stronger universities have an opportunity to charge what they believe the market will bear, relying on their reputation to attract clients. The weaker universities have less room for manoeuvre. In a few cases already burdened by debt, and sometimes with falling enrolment, they must estimate whether in the final analysis the government — any government — will let them go to the wall.

The fall of a university would have an impact in any community and could not fail to have negative consequences even for the most anti-intellectual government. For that reason, if for no other, we assume that governments will attempt to manage events so that actual closures will be avoided. But mergers, amputations, and other forms of reduction are certainly in the cards. Some are well in train, as in Nova Scotia, Saskatchewan, and, perhaps, Ontario.

Mergers, à la Nova Scotia, and amputations, à la Ohio, are a fairly rational response to limited budgets and scarce taxpayer resources. They require a certain amount of political courage and administrative skill, which makes them, from a government's point of view, not very desirable even where feasible. Another possibility is salary reductions and other forms of internal economy. These remedies are politically saleable outside the universities, even if inside they depress morale and stimulate inefficiency. There are risks, however.

Through a decade and more of underfunding, universities have relied on the fact that most of their faculty cannot afford to go else-where. There is a limited market at the top, where a few prominent professors in alluring fields can make the move — Soviet studies in the 1980s, certain forms of economics, some varieties of public policy stud-ies, and even a few practitioners of Canadian history. From time to time universities underfund so badly, or so noticeably, that their faculty pull up stakes. Such was the case with the University of British Columbia in the mid-1980s. Faculty fled in all directions — to the United States, elsewhere in Canada, anywhere — to escape a system that systemati-cally undervalued their services.

Where do university teachers stand economically, relative to other Canadians? According to the 1991 census, university teaching is the tenth most lucrative occupation in Canada, behind judges, doctors, lawyers, "general managers and other senior officials," pilots, and chi-ropractors. (They may actually be eleventh, behind professional ath-letes, but there aren't enough of this last category to be statistically significant.) They currently make about as much as policemen, and considerably more than elementary and secondary schoolteachers.[13]

Tenth place may look promising, but inevitably such statistics will affect individual choice on whether to enter a given occupation. Canada's 41,000 lawyers (1990 figures) make, on average, 25 percent more than Canada's professors; and Canada's 129,000 "general man-agers and other senior officials" are about 8 percent up. These figures are based on an aging (i.e., more senior and higher-paid) professoriate and a notorious glut of younger and ill-paid lawyers. It is not surpris-ing that many more intelligent and able young Canadians choose the other "learned professions" or cast their lot with large private-sector companies. And it is not surprising that many choose to emigrate.

---

13. Statistics Canada, "Average Earnings of Full-Year, Full-Time Working Men and Women in Ten Highest and Ten Lowest Paying Occupations, 1990," The Daily, 13 April 1993, 86. Relatively speaking, and in constant 1990 dollars, university teachers reached a modest peak around 1980, and are currently on the average making less than they did in 1970. Statistics Canada, Education Quarterly Review 2 (summer 1995): 13.

It is possible that Canadian universities and their provincial pay-masters will so mismanage their cutbacks as to make Canada a happy hunting ground for recruiters from abroad. True, these hunters will be interested only in the most prestigious professors and the best-funded researchers. Certainly, they will discourage talented and well-trained people from staying in Canada. Nor should we expect the private sector to compensate for what the universities cannot offer. Many newly minted PhDs are already leaving for better-paying "high tech" jobs. The *Toronto Star* sounded the alarm in August 1996: "Double-digit growth in information-technology industries and the broadened horizons of global trade are making borders irrelevant for the most skilled and the most mobile workers." Though talented Canadians have always been lured to the larger and richer economy to the south, "the drain is accelerating," according to Canadian high-tech firms.[14] This particular Canadian export, highly trained people, is flourishing.

Comparative salaries are also instructive. The University of Toronto stands first in pay scales among Canadian universities, yet its salaries suffer by comparison with even mediocre American universities, especially when the Canadian dollar is exchanged for American currency. At the top of the American scale, say at Harvard, the difference is even wider. Full professors there earn $120,000 a year ($162,000 Canadian at the rates prevailing in October 1996). They receive an interest-free loan to buy a house, and in the United States mortgage interest is tax deductible, making this latter transaction free of tax.

But Harvard is Harvard. What about other American universities, closer to the University of Toronto or other Canadian universities in standing and history? The University of Pennsylvania, an Ivy League school, dispenses $132,000 (Canadian funds) to its full professors and $76,000 to its assistant professors. The University of Chicago and New York University, not Ivy League schools but universities with a firm reputation, are in the same salary ballpark. The University of Michigan

---

14. Adam Myers, "Top Grads Go South," *Toronto Star*, 24 August 1996.

and Berkeley are less rewarding, at $116,000 and $118,000 for full professors and around $68,000 for assistant professors.[15] The comparable University of Toronto salaries are $81,000 for full professors and $44,000 for assistant professors. For the brightest and best among Canadian faculty, the brain drain flows north to south as fast as it can.

There have been some wrong-headed suggestions that we cut off the transborder flow of scholars and researchers. Those trained in Canada, paid for by Canadian taxes, should stay in Canada, according to this argument. This policy has a wealth of experience behind it — serfdom, peonage, and slavery. Most recently, it was tried by the old Soviet Union, which used it as just another means to keep its intelligentsia in line. Even with such a recommendation, it is unlikely that Canadian governments would go so far as to abrogate their subjects' freedom to move. After all, most of these scholars can't, or won't. They will just stay and become frustrated, or be assisted into early retirement.

The effect of cutbacks is demoralizing. The first is a transfer of power. Universities are theoretically collegial bodies, but colleagues are not very good at administering pain, and the burden of reductions tends to be borne by the administration. The scramble for funds among divisions or departments leads to increasingly restrictive budgetary controls. There is more bureaucracy to manage less money, with more forms to fill out amid appeals for "accountability" — meaning still more forms to bring faculty into "compliance."[16]

In a very limited sense the effect is beneficial. Certain forms of waste are done away with, driven underground, or forced off the budget in search of private sponsorship. But "tight control" over money

15. "Are U of T Salaries Competitive with Our Peer Universities?" University of Toronto Faculty Association, *News Bulletin*, 19 February 1997.

16. We do not wish to suggest this is the only reason why university bureaucracies have grown over the twenty years. There are many reasons: functions formerly performed by faculty which, under pressure of more students, have had to be turned over to civil servants; and a political climate that favours regulation and restriction in all areas of life.

means just that — a world designed by and run for accountants. And accountability sometimes means just the opposite — decisions exported to committees in which no one individual can be held responsible. Individual initiative, which functions best without controls, is lost.

If universities are unlikely to be closed, faculties and departments can be. The University of Toronto, the nation's largest, has proposed to concentrate its resources on its most successful programs. This program has already been tried at Alberta and now, with Alberta's ex-president at the helm, at the University of Western Ontario. Consortiums, amalgamations, specialization, and concentration are all sensible in theory and certainly in line with the approved aim of efficiency. It is arguable that without the reality of government reductions, none of them would have happened. Even in the best of circumstances, however, budgetary reductions cut broadly and crudely.

Take the University of Alberta. The university was presented by the Alberta government with a package demanding a 21 percent budgetary reduction over three years. It met this reality in three ways. First, employees took a 5 percent pay cut. Second, tuition rose, over three years, from $1600 to $3000. Third, 200 faculty positions were abolished. Inside the university, money was reallocated. Less prominent programs, those judged less successful, shrank. The arts and science faculties maintained their position, but only by taking in more students. Other faculties, such as education, were not as lucky, while the university's high-flying professional faculties fared relatively well — their funding was cut, but by a lesser percentage.

Then there was the University of Waterloo. It jumped to reduce costs in the fall of 1995. Correctly identifying senior salaries as a very large part of its budgetary problem, the administration devised a generous early retirement package and mailed it out to all faculty. The result has been variously interpreted. Some commentators hail Waterloo as brilliantly successful. A large number of professors took the offer. Among full-time faculty, numbers fell from 806 in 1992–93, to 767 in 1995–96, to 640 in 1996–97. Their places may be filled by younger professors, who are also cheaper, or the retirees may not be replaced — cheaper still. But surveying these results, it is hard to escape the sense that among those who left were some of the university's most successful and most prominent professors. Some departments, such as civil engineering and psychology, gave substance to Waterloo's claim to be first in Canada. Psychology has now lost almost all its Fellows of the Royal Society of Canada, to use one measure.

In the cash-scarce environment of the mid-1990s, government retreat from funding may have other implications. With government less willing to act as the ultimate dispenser of funds to all, there is less pressure on universities to cooperate. This may seem to contradict the pressure by governments on universities to share, cooperate, amalgamate, and rationalize. But in the short term there may well be advantage in abandoning cooperation and adopting competition as the *modus operandi* of higher education.

This trend is already apparent in requests for differential funding. But differential funding — a form of university merit pay — is not the only recourse. With funds diminishing, one way to shore up the government grant is to admit more students. This resource is most readily available to stronger universities, which by lowering entrance standards 1 or 2 percent can keep their own enrolments high, or even send them higher. Of course, the price is paid by less prestigious universities, and some universities as a result are not far from the financial wall.

These circumstances may seem depressing, but they may well be eclipsed by the Ontario government's July 1996 white paper on higher education. The Harris government is committed to privatization because of the incidental revenue that sales of government assets will provide and because it genuinely believes that better government is lesser government. It must also consider the effects on provincial finances of drastically smaller federal contributions to the Ontario treasury, including the end of federal cash transfers for higher education.

The white paper set out a whole new context for discussing higher education. Higher education must rely less on government. Drawing less from the public, universities may be obliged to turn private — by privatizing themselves, free of government grants, or by forming "partnerships" with private business. While professing a general commitment to education in all its forms, the white paper zeroed in on practical education — education for jobs — both in providing new skills for the Ontario workforce and in bolstering the province's industrial effort. This emphasis had ominous implications for anyone working in impractical subjects, from pure science to political science to classics, and it reminded universities, if any reminding was needed, that they needed alternative sources of funding.

Raising tuition was one way of getting funds. Seeking donations from alumni, charitable contributions, or grants-in-aid from corporations was another avenue to explore. Much was made of Canada's higher taxes and propensity to rely on government for social and educational spending, which meant there was much in Canadians' historical behaviour that would have to be changed, if universities were to hope for voluntary gifts. To do it, universities hired fundraisers and paid them at market rates. The University of Toronto, for example, paid its fundraiser $250,000, more than the president and more than anyone else in the university.

Occasional grants from the private sector, or from charitable foundations, are one thing. Regular, sustainable income is, we suspect, quite another. The charitable sector in Canada is limited in its gift-giving potential, and corporate donations are circumscribed, not infinite. Nor do Canadian universities have large endowments.

It is impossible to escape the conclusion that some form of government financing is inescapable if, and it is an if, Canadians wish to have, and thus pay for, a few first-class universities. It is equally hard to escape the conclusion that the provincial governments are not the ones to do it. Some will not do it because they have not got the money — Saskatchewan, New Brunswick, or Newfoundland, for example. Some will not do it because they are confused, and uncertain whether it would not be better to appease the gods of political correctness by demolishing what they have — as in British Columbia. And some like Ontario and Alberta simply take a dim and unfriendly view of the university enterprise. Their constituencies, they know all too well, do not lie in ivy-covered halls. Momentum and inertia are probably the universities' best guardians in those two provinces.

For the best Canadian universities there may eventually be some financial relief at the end of a long and dreary funding tunnel. The components of that relief will not be prescribed by the apostles of privatization, however. If we accept that tuition will play a larger role in university finance than it does at present, that university endowments will be encouraged to grow, and that private giving in various forms will increase, there will still be a shortfall in university finance.

Universities can meet the shortfall in several ways. They may become differentiated and specialized in function as well as objective. Some universities will cost less because they do less, or fulfil their mission more cheaply. Others will cost more, and that more will have to be clearly identified as research. The provinces are unfortunately not likely to wish or be able to fund research either generously or intelligently.

Research brings us back to the rationale originally adopted by the federal government to support universities, back in the 1950s. Research in those days was considered a national asset, and universities were seen as the place to do it. Relying on its duty to promote trade and hence the economy, and justifying that by appealing to national security, the federal government gave Canadian universities the necessary funds to grow and compete for over forty years. Like university finance in general, the federal aid was spread too broadly and did not do enough good where it would have counted most — in the stronger universities. Times have changed, but the circumstances of research have not. The provinces have demonstrated that they will not step into the breach created by the withdrawal of federal funds. What, under those circumstances, can be done?

Asking the federal government to get back into university finance will seem fanciful — but it is the least fanciful and the least obnoxious alternative available to Canadians. Federal systems exist so that different levels of government do what they can do best. Experience shows that provincial governments are not well suited to operate universities — universities that they will not fund. If Canada has a future, and we

hope and believe it does, it must include a restored national commitment to university excellence.

We sometimes argue that we have governments in order to make
choices, often difficult choices. Political choices have to do with the
allocation of resources among competing groups. In the recent prosperous past we avoided choices by funding everybody, even though the
money for such a policy was not really there. The danger in the neo-
conservative 1990s is that we will avoid choice by funding nobody, even
though there is some money which, if used in a concentrated manner
on limited objectives, could still produce a level of higher education
that would really meet the competition we are already receiving.

The fault is our own. Our administrative culture, private and public, thrives on choice-avoidance. We export decisions to panels and
commissions and pass endless hours discussing process rather than outcomes. We pretend that choices do not really have to be made, ignoring
the reality of limited resources which, if used wisely, economically, and
efficiently, can benefit all Canadians. True, a proper use of our limited
resources for universities will not benefit all the governments of
Canada, but we must be brave and face up to the possibility that, in
some circumstances, one government is better and cheaper than ten.
After all, what have we got to lose?

There are other alternatives. Canada has already shown that it can
do a good job exporting people. A declining, parochial university system, starving but in place, will help secure that future. It is not the
future of a nation or, in the longer term, of even a country.

Chapter 3

The Collapse of Standards:
The Decline and Fall of Absolutely Everything

THE TERM "WORLD CLASS" has been a favourite in the 1990s, and Canadians seem to like the idea. Toronto, at least until the recession of 1991, was a world-class city; Vancouver is one now, and Montreal used to be. Various Canadian animals — beavers, reindeer, caribou perhaps — are world class because in these natural products Canadians set the standard.

Canada is world class in education, too. Canadians spent more money per university student in 1991 — the last year for which global figures are available — than any other country. That year, Canadians spent more ($8359) than the Germans ($7504) or the Japanese ($5675). This comparison is impressive, and it testifies to Canadians' commitment to learning.

So it should follow that Canada's students should be world class too, studying in world-class institutions offering world-class learning. And, because Canada's universities are publicly financed, as many Canadians as possible should study there. After all, with the money that flows in, Canada and its universities should be competitive with the best in the world — in facilities, in salaries, and, of course, in prestige. The answer to these propositions is, well, no. No to any of them and no to all.

Why not? The answer is twofold. First, our politicians have managed a "world-class" problem with parochial solutions. Education is about jobs and local pride. This is the philosophy of the public works project: grand in concept, transcendental in the expectations created, and meagre only in the funding required to maintain the edifice. Much of Canada's higher education statistics can be explained in these terms. But there is more: the curse of Canadian regionalism. Ten provinces? Ten universities! Regions within provinces? Give each of them a university, east, west, north, south, and then subdivide according to taste. Why should it matter? There are students for all of them. And indeed there are, if you lower the entrance standards a grade or two or, better still, abolish the entrance standard. Expensive universities demand that we have large numbers of students.

Second, Canada has a wonderful location and glorious scenery, but in the academic world it is, still, lagging. Every time a Canadian university approaches the big leagues, as McGill did in the earlier part of this century, circumstances conspire to bat it down. Canada has always had to try just a little harder to get itself taken seriously, and that is as true among universities as in other fields. Usually, however, we don't try harder, and as a result we have trouble competing.

This little secret is not much talked about around the universities. Sometimes it pops up, when Canadian universities try to contend with the University of Chicago for an economist, or when they lose some of their finest faculty to Berkeley or Harvard. Other times it's money or the weather. But as often as not it's something else — reputation, the sense of being connected, or the idea that by going south you are moving from Class A to the Major Leagues.

Can it be that, for all the money, Canadian universities are not measuring up? Well, yes. Does it really matter? Shouldn't we shrug and mumble something about "the price of being Canadian"? Canadians like to think of themselves as modest, aw-shucks folks, so why not be modest in achievement too? This, at least, we have accomplished in higher education. As Peter Leslie, a prominent Canadian economist, put it a decade ago, "In Canadian education, the main emphasis has been on minimum standards and universal accessibility rather than on building universities with a world reputation." Leslie was right then, and even more right now.

Some people have noticed. Peter Godsoe, chief executive officer of the Bank of Nova Scotia, observed in 1996 that he was "unaware of any country outside Canada that does not have two or three world-class institutions." He exaggerated. Of course, there are plenty of countries that do not have world-class institutions. Burkina Faso, Paraguay, Mauritius, Albania — there are scores of nations huddled at the bottom of the education league. But among the countries with which Canada usually compares itself — the countries of the First World, of the Organization for Economic Cooperation and Development, of the Group of 7 — the case for Canada is shakier. And among the countries that most closely resemble Canada in language, social structure, and economy, the Canadian idol topples despite the endless sacrifices of money offered before it.

Why worry? Canada's universities have been around a long time. They are still there, still solid, no matter what carping critics may say. And certainly there is precedent, if not merit, in this argument.

In an older Canada, a very much older Canada, universities were founded as part of the same cultural imperative that governed the foundation of universities in Western Europe, South America, or the United States. They made learning available in the forest and on the prairies. Learning was an essential component of democracy and society, as well as a building block for the economy. American politicians took pride in erecting "the" state university, in Michigan, in Kansas, in California. Across the border, with a twenty-year lag, Canadian politicians did the same thing. Given a 30 percent gap in standard of living, the Canadians were slower and more modest; and given that Canada was a colony in the larger British Empire, rather than a stand-alone country like the United States, Canadians subsumed some of their educational ambitions in the great universities of the empire, Oxford and Cambridge. But they always kept an eye on the United States and, over time, followed American fashions and practices.

The Americans and the British understood the role of universities. The university has always been the training ground, "the place," Ursula Franklin said, "society put aside to train, to equip, to brainwash, to educate those and the next generation of those who were supposed to run the ship of state." That is why, in the United States, for example, there are a number of élite universities (such as Harvard or MIT), a large number of very good schools that range across the whole sphere of learning from medicine to classics (such as Duke), numerous specialized universities or liberal arts colleges with smaller student bodies that give first-class educations in their own area (such as CalTech or Oberlin), and a huge array of lesser institutions that strive for greatness (such as Boston College) or that make no pretence of anything but to cater to mediocre students (such as the mythical Podunk State). Britain and France, in different ways, have the same gradations, and so too do a dozen other nations whose institutions have emerged from the same traditions.

But Canada is different, and the main indicator of this uniqueness has been the policy of accessibility. By the mid-twentieth century, a university education was beginning to be recognized as the key to personal and economic success. In the atmosphere of rising expectations, a Bachelor's degree was the ticket to executive positions, to a teaching job, or to officer rank in the military. At every level of society, education was a panacea, a guarantor of place and preference. Canadian universities, however, were small and few in number, the percentage of high school leavers proceeding to higher education was low, and the perception persisted that only the children of the wealthy could readily go to university.

In an increasingly egalitarian nation, this élitism was unacceptable. It was especially so after the Second World War, when politicians noticed that their American cousins were expanding their universities and colleges. More and more Americans went to universities: many more than in Canada both absolutely and proportionately. Ontario, Canada's largest and richest province, took the lead. Leslie Frost, the shrewd Conservative premier from 1948 to 1961 who had an eye for what the voters wanted, began to press for expansion of the Ontario system. "I think that no person in this country who has the potential to make good in the university world and the things that lead from the university," he said, "should be denied that education." That was entirely proper — in a meritocratic democracy all Canadians were entitled to rise as far as their talents could take them, and class ought never to be the determinant.

Five years later, however, Frost's successor, John Robarts, began to push his province down a different path. The standard for admission to university, Robarts said, "should be moderate and reasonable such as to enable the average student to proceed to a degree....55 and 60%, dependent on the type of course," he explained, should define what he meant by an average student. A grade of 60 percent three decades ago meant rather more than 60 percent today; even so, 60 percent was a mediocre grade, and the floodgates yawned wide in approval. The Ontario government, and the governments in every province, began to demand that their universities admit the mediocre students. Very soon it was done: every qualified applicant with the money to pay tuition or the capacity to get a student loan was entitled to a place at a university, though not necessarily at the institution or in the program of first choice. In other words, "more students good, fewer students bad," a slogan brayed out with Orwellian repetitiveness. The result: by 1993, 40 percent of Canadians between the ages of twenty-five and sixty-four had completed some form of tertiary education — the highest level among developed nations. (The U.S. figure was 36 percent; the British, 16; the Australian, 31; and the Swedish, 23.)

Making accessibility the prime motive had positive and negative results.The bad news first: there is no single university in Canada that is truly outstanding. None can truly claim to draw the best students in Canada or to offer an array of programs that are all or even predominantly first class. All that can be said is that one university may have a good law school, but be weak in graduate programs in the humanities; another might be strong in engineering, but weak in the social sciences; some, in fact, live on their reputations from long-gone days.

But there was some good news, too. The increase in the number of universities and community colleges, and the number of places available, meant that, in theory if not always in practice, higher education became more readily available to those who were not wealthy or middle class. More immigrants, women, and working-class offspring could now go to university, something that was wholly positive.[1]

Improving access was a positive good, but perhaps one that took a wrong turn along the way. Opening the doors to those whose high school grades suggested either a lack of application or a lack of brain power was an error. There were many exceptions in the brilliant late bloomers who were duds at seventeen but near-geniuses at twenty-three, people who likely might have found their way to higher education in any case. But the net effect of accessibility carried to extremes was wholly predictable — admitting all comers, and letting most of them stay at university until graduation, guaranteed that the quality of Canadian higher education could not rise above the mediocre.

In effect, Canada's universities quickly found themselves at a crossroads. Was the university intended to provide a high-quality education to those who were most likely to benefit from it? Or were universities there as just another sorting mechanism for the labour market, a system designed to separate the white-collar workers from the blue? Canadian universities predictably and characteristically dithered and decided to go in neither direction — they reduced the quality of education offered to those who were the brightest in society and, instead, made themselves into an ineffective sorting mechanism. The result is that, today, many students drift along, boring themselves, the hard-working students, and their instructors with their utter lack of interest in anything but sex, soap operas, the Blue Jays, and the Grizzlies. There's no job at the end of university, the Generation X lament goes, so why work? And, of course, there is more than a little truth in it.

---

1. Typically, however, Canadians have carried this accessibility policy to extremes. Law schools like the University of Ottawa, for example, have put in place equity programs to increase the numbers of places for women, men and women of colour, and aboriginals, and to deny access to the qualified white males whose grades would otherwise have allowed them entry. The law schools say it is all a matter of defining what constitutes qualifications and that an aboriginal woman, for one, has important qualifications stemming from her different perspective. There are no fixed quotas, but the numbers of various groups admitted seem surprisingly consistent year after year. For us, a quota is a quota is a quota — and it's wrong.

Why did the universities not cry halt? In a word — money. Larger enrolments and a commitment to accessibility meant that the universities could make a strong case for ever-higher government funding, especially as most provinces adopted a per capita financing scheme. Where no such financing scheme existed, larger numbers still offered the best argument for more in public moneys. And, of course, provincial governments had their own political objectives to serve by opening higher education to the people. In the per capita funding provinces, one Arts undergraduate was ordinarily worth $X, one engineering student was worth $2X, one dentistry student was $5X, and one PhD student $6X. The result of enrolment-based funding was a badly clogged system, with classrooms full of students who were not intellectually suited to handle the university experience and challenge.

As late as the 1950s, first-year courses were designed to chase away the students who could not be expected to secure a degree. "Look around you," deans used to say to their incoming students. "The people on both sides of you won't be here when you graduate." And it was largely true. Large numbers of incoming students did not graduate, the victims of a policy that deliberately discouraged those who could not make the grade. There were exceptions, of course, in the ones who coasted through on "gentlemen's Cs," relying on charm and Daddy's money to keep the academic wolf from the door. It is admittedly hard to compare, but standards may well have been higher then than today — though there were always some courses where neither work nor intelligence was required.

What is different in the 1990s is that the university full-time student population of a half-million is some five times greater than it was four decades ago, though the national population has only doubled. The part-time student enrolment has also doubled in the last quarter-century and, while thousands of students still drop out, it is harder than ever to fail, though surprising numbers, as we shall see, manage to do so. In some institutions, almost literally, the only requirement for a degree is to be present and to turn in the assignments. According to the Organization for Economic Cooperation and Development's data, 10 percent of Canadian university graduates are functionally illiterate in a population where 47 percent of the entire population are similarly handicapped, able to read only the simplest of texts or unable to read at all. Presumably the graduates' assignments were never monitored closely by their instructors. Professors have obviously lowered their expectations and their standards. They teach and grade for the median student, but because a large part of the increase in enrolment came — and continues to come — from students at the bottom end of the academic scale, the median continues to fall.

Without sounding too categorical, we believe that standards are falling in the university, although the process is far from uniform. Admittedly, there is almost no hard data. Short of comparing essays and the grades received for the same topic in the same course over a generation, something that cannot be done, most of the evidence is inevitably anecdotal. John Osborne, an educational psychologist at the University of Alberta, lamented the aggressive ignorance of current students: "It is easier for students to expect their professors to reduce standards than it is for them to make the effort to upgrade themselves."

The faculty, naturally enough, swim with the tide. If you grade high, no one will complain; if you mark toughly, students use the university's array of quasi-legal procedures to grieve their B, when they absolutely must have an A to get into the MBA program. "Who wants to ruin June," one faculty member said, "being dragged through an appeal process by a student who can't take B for an answer?" Not many faculty, especially if the appeal process results in an order that a new examination be set and marked. Even worse — we hesitate to suggest this complication, but it is true — if the complaining student is a person of colour or from the opposite sex, the threat of a racial discrimination or a sexual harassment complaint comes unbidden to every terrified faculty member's mind. As one Toronto emeritus professor lamented: "Is there anyone within academe who cares?" In the absence of hard data, no one seems to care very much.

But there is one area where there is no doubt: standards vary widely among programs. At the University of Alberta, for example, nearly 80 percent of the students in the Faculty of Education scored grades equivalent to an A, while less than 40 percent of engineering students did the same. An engineering professor, bitterly protesting, stated bluntly that either education students were twice as bright as student engineers or his colleagues in education lived "in a dream world" that cheated prospective employers. Of course, engineers who build bridges must know what they are doing; there is apparently no need for those who will educate the country's children to be graded with equivalent severity.

Yet calls for performance indicators or for national or provincial quality standards are rejected by faculty associations and administrators alike. When the Klein government in Alberta imposed seventeen performance indicators on the province's universities (including completion rates, success of graduates in employment, and the success of students transferring among institutions) and pledged to base a portion of university funding on performance, the initial response to the Tory beancounters' efforts ranged from unease to outrage — though the university administrations, sensing that they had no choice, quickly decided to work with Edmonton to ensure that the standards were "fair."

Attempts to measure standards in the universities, to weigh teaching performance in a serious way, or to assess the quality of research are seen as a threat. Faculty associations and their provincial organizations, staring budget cuts in the face, worry that provincially imposed performance indicators will lead only to attempts by their administrations to speed up the production line and cram more students into classrooms. Administrators fret that credible indicators and standards will draw invidious comparisons between Lethbridge and Alberta, or St Mary's and Dalhousie, with serious impact on their schools.

Maclean's magazine, however, has stepped in where provincial governments and universities have feared to tread, as its annual university rankings assemble vast quantities of data and compare schools against each other. The reason that Canadians are beginning to accept that some universities may be better than others is almost wholly attributable to the efforts of a magazine. Each November since 1992, *Maclean's* has ranked virtually all universities in the country, assessing everything from the dormitories to the laboratories, the libraries to the faculty's success in securing research grants, the percentage of high-grade-average students entering and the percentage of students graduating. The ratings have had their impact, in substantial part because they were all that existed, apart from a few books, most of which presented the most anodyne of data. The public obviously wanted something, anything, that made comparisons, and *Maclean's* gave it to them.

The ratings were sadly flawed. Initially listing every university in a head-to-head competition, the huge University of Toronto against small Acadia, for example, the rankings were a classic case of comparing apples to oranges to peanuts. *Maclean's*, the universities complained in 1993, "gives the impression that it is possible to measure excellence and quality reliably by developing rather simple quantitative measures." Even so, the institutions that ranked high strutted and preened. McGill University felt its first place was justifiable, though few academics elsewhere in Canada would have agreed. The Montreal university, punished for years by Quebec's anglophone-hating governments, seemed to most knowledgeable observers to be living on reputation alone. Tiny Mount Allison, located in Sackville, New Brunswick, also ranked well — despite an underpaid faculty in revolt and a lean library. Apparently, the number of dormitory beds per registered student counted highly in the *Maclean's* mix.

More recent *Maclean's* ratings have been refined substantially and new categories of a more comparable nature have developed. Even so, there is no doubt that the magazine still tends to favour the smaller, self-styled élite institutions and that it measures inputs much better than it does the outcomes — the quality and level of skills of the students who graduate.[2] Similarly, university administrators complain

---

2. Not that the universities themselves ever measure the outcome of the education they proffer; a York University study in 1996, for example, found no strong link between grades and the acquired skills employers want. The author of the study, Paul Grayson, took an implicit shot at *Maclean's*: "For example, one university having more student residences than another means little unless a connection is made to the impact on student learning."

that *Maclean's* is still very weak in its assessments of graduate studies and in measuring faculty research efforts in quantity, let alone quality. And if, as we suggest, most universities are strong in some areas, *Maclean's* ratings fail to take this factor into account. Some presidents and deans (and not just those from low-ranked universities) bluntly consider *Maclean's* more a part of the problem than a contributor to any solution. At the University of Waterloo, for example, the departure of large numbers of senior faculty following the early retirement buyout in 1995 has led to no major change in *Maclean's* rating of the university.

Nonetheless, if those universities at the top in *Maclean's* might not have been the right ones, they were at least pleased. Those at the bottom were uniformly convinced they had been betrayed, slandered, and abused. Their administrations raged, sulked, and, in some cases, refused to cooperate in the next year's rankings. Their students, perhaps blithely assuming that Lethbridge, Brandon, or Laurentian was the equivalent of Queen's or UBC, were disabused. At Ottawa's Carleton University, for example, the university's policy of allowing in students with lower high school averages than the Ontario norm was revealed before the nation to have a price in the form of a very low rank, forty-fourth out of forty-six schools rated. The situation was perhaps not quite as bleak as that rank suggested — incompetent administrators had given *Maclean's* the wrong figures in some key areas. Subsequent in-house studies, however, demonstrated that the institution was in terrible shape, and, before long, Carleton professors, their professional standing in jeopardy, were up in arms, fighting the president for the imposition of standards and for programs tailored to brighter students. Carleton was going about the hard task of turning itself around in the right ways, but even so its 1996–97 first-year enrolments were down substantially (from 6442 in 1993 to 3945 in 1996), with harmful effects on its budgetary position. Many faculty — and possibly some entire departments and programs — faced layoffs and closures. Carleton, of course, was not alone in its plight. Other Canadian universities had turned themselves into slightly advanced high schools, their faculties doing more baby-sitting and spoon-feeding than teaching and research.

The implications of this collapse of standards are, or should be, clear. Professors do not enjoy teaching bad students, just as the brightest students bitterly resent being made to sit in overcrowded classrooms stuffed full of dullards. Good students need smaller classes that can challenge them, but such classes are not to be found — unless the university or department has a tough honours program, and most no longer do. Honours programs smack of élitism, and élitism is out of favour in academe every bit as much as in Canadian society generally. The result — and there is some evidence to support this claim in surveys of Ontario Scholars leaving after first year at some Ontario universities — is that large numbers of the best students drop out or go to British or American universities, the victims of Canadian university terminal boredom. This loss doesn't appear to occur in professional schools, but it is a serious problem nonetheless. No nation can long afford to see many of its ablest students rejecting learning, education, or training. It is a disaster in the making for Canada.

The weak students do not seem to enjoy the university experience either. Indeed, the attrition rates among marginal students admitted to higher education, thanks to the policy of open accessibility, are staggeringly high. What should be asked is whether universities are doing such students any favour by admitting them. There are high and increasing financial costs in attending university, and the dropout gains little except debt. There are also emotional costs that might well be suffered by students who discover that they simply cannot handle the work. These students should never be admitted. But they are, the universities implicitly saying, "We know you're not qualified (and you know it, too), but it's your money and and if you want to give it a shot..." It's also public money in huge quantities, of course, and it's being wasted.

There is another mitigating factor here. With tuition rising, large and increasing numbers of students are forced to hold a part-time job to pay for their education. Worse yet, student debt is also increasing rapidly, saddling graduates — who may expect trouble finding work — with a future of more scrimping. To work two days or three evenings a week is almost certain to affect performance in class and minimize the amount of time that can be found to research a sociology paper or work on a math problem. Students have always held jobs; the sense now exists that more are doing so and that the need to work is hurting performance more than ever before and, predictably, leading to higher drop-out rates.

The attrition rates are very high. At Carleton, where rebellious faculty fighting the administration to raise standards collected the best data available at any university in Canada, approximately two-thirds of honours BA program students were found to graduate — but over a ten-year period, rather than the four years usually taken to complete the degree. In the pass BA program, the courses that usually attract less able students, "very few graduate no matter how long you wait." In 1991–92, 60 percent of pass BA students who registered in the first year failed to register in the second year; in honours programs, the attrition rate incredibly was nearly 80 percent. Rising tuition fees will likely force more students, including some good ones, to drop out.

It wasn't only Carleton that had such numbers. In the province of Quebec, only 30 percent of part-time students receive a degree, and half of those full-time students who switch programs fail to graduate. At Calgary, Fredericton's St Thomas University, and the University of Winnipeg, according to Maclean's 1995 data, respectively only 57.2, 57.2, and 45.3 percent of second-year students graduate — and those data do not take into account the very substantial numbers of students who fail to complete first-year courses. The University of Manitoba argues that its "student continuation rate" — the number of first-year students going on to second year — should be 90 percent. If it falls below 90 percent, the university investigates why with a sophisticated and expensive tracking system. The university is looking to see if poor program quality drives students away; it apparently does not investigate to determine if poor program quality lets the unqualified continue onwards. It should.

In Montreal, Dawson College, an English-language CEGEP or university-preparatory college, discovered that its history department was failing too many students. At Ministry of Education orders, the department was told in no uncertain terms in 1996 to lower its standards and pass more students. To ensure that this outcome was achieved, the instructors were directed to assign no more than 200 pages of reading per term per course. Twenty years ago, it used to be the norm in history courses to assign from 125 to 200 pages a week.

Predictably, the overall drop-out rates are highest among the very students targeted in the push for accessibility. In the late 1980s at the University of New Brunswick, just under three in four of the students admitted with high school grades between 60 and 65 percent were required to withdraw or were placed on probation; for students with high school grades 10 percent higher, 39 percent were in academic jeopardy — still a staggeringly high percentage.

One rationale, as we have seen, was to open up the university to the hitherto disadvantaged — the immigrants, the poor, women, and other historically maltreated groups. The universities, pushed by the provincial governments and the changing composition of the Canadian population, were getting involved in social engineering. And the result? At Carleton University, the one Ontario institution that has made a special effort to open its doors to those who "are not able to enter programs with limited enrolments [higher standards, as measured by grades] at Carleton or elsewhere," the school's student body remained surprisingly unaltered, despite the best of intentions. According to a 1994 assessment of the results of the university's open admissions policy, Carleton's students were disproportionately male and middle class when compared with other institutions. In Quebec, a 1985 study noted the same thing: "The recent democratization of the higher education system benefited the groups already attending... by offering a greater guarantee of access...to the children of the middle and upper classes." But if Carleton failed to change the social composition of its student body, it was remarkably successful in lowering standards, just as its faculty had claimed. In 1993, more than half of the incoming students had averages under 70 percent, and the university harvested an astonishing seven in ten of all Ontario high school leaving students with grades below 65 percent. Five years earlier, Carleton took in only 44 percent of these students. Loading up the first year program with huge numbers of weak students meant that Carleton took in only 852 fewer students in 1993 than the University of Toronto, Canada's largest university. Predictably, Gresham's Law took hold. Just as bad money drives out good, so too do bad students drive out the excellent: in 1993, Carleton also admitted the smallest share of Ontario Scholars (students with averages of 80 percent or higher).

We are not picking on Carleton University. It is not very different from the other universities of Ontario and Canada, and it has many first-class scholars in its faculty ranks. But government policies and a succession of bad decisions created a difficult, perhaps impossible, situation for the Ottawa institution. Low standards corrupt; the lowest standards corrupt absolutely. In late October 1996, trying to respond to the crisis it faced, Carleton's administration announced a major restructuring that aimed to reinforce the university's undoubted strengths in areas such as public administration, history, international relations, and journalism, and to cut where it is weakest. We can only wish these efforts success.

What all the universities desperately need — and cannot secure — are admission standards that mean something. Traditionally, admission standards have been used to identify those applicants with the greatest chance of success; to guarantee equitable treatment for admission to limited enrolment programs and for scholarships; to certify that a student has the requisite preparation for admission to a specific program; and to ensure that the student has the general education expected of a high school graduate. Now, however, and for some years past, admission standards have been engineered to allow almost anyone access to university, whether or not that student has any chance of succeeding. In essence, the universities' treatment of high school leaving grades has become only a method of controlling student numbers.

If enrolments drop, requirements decline not because the university believes that the students will do well, but simply to increase the pool of potential customers. When applications are on the rise, however, the cut-off point for admission will ordinarily rise in step, not because the university hopes to attract better students, but simply to control the numbers admitted. For example, at the University of Calgary, when applications in the mid-1990s fell by some 3 percent, the university promptly created 450 spaces for students and proposed to fill them by reducing the admission standard from 73 percent to 65 percent for General Studies students. Given a special government grant to take in the students, the university denied that it was lowering standards; instead, the associate vice-president of student affairs claimed that Calgary had decided it had been turning away too many students who had the potential to do well, but the results — poorer performance among those with the lower grades — did not bear the administrator out. Still, as a York University associate dean said a few years before: "Is a university which enables a student with a seventy percent high school average to reach her full potential any less excellent than one which specializes in the education of Ontario Scholars?" The answer ought to be obvious, and it should have been one that caused a storm of controversy. Instead, the dean was right: in the eyes of government, there is no significant difference.

In fact, it may no longer be possible to link high school leaving grades and standards. Every time a university raises its entrance mark, high school leaving grades mysteriously rise by roughly the same number. What else could be expected? Teachers have been trained to be sensitive, to reward interest rather than achievement, and to work to allay student anxieties. Few provinces any longer have provincewide examinations to provide a quality check, and the resulting system where each and every school sets its own exams has had the predictable results. Why should anyone assume that 2300 grade 12 teachers in some three hundred Saskatchewan high schools will have the same standards? And how can a Nova Scotia university, faced with an application from a British Columbia student, have any sense of how that student's grades and training compare with those of a boy from Lunenberg or a girl from Meat Cove?[3] The simple truth is that two virtually equal students can have radically different grades, depending on the high school they attend.

There is a glimmer of hope. Alberta tests students on a provincewide basis in most subjects, and Calgary high schools recently bragged that they had topped the charts in nine of ten categories. After years of avoiding demeaning comparisons of any kind, for schools in Canada to boast about high achievement is a breakthrough.

It's none too soon. Let there be no doubt that the quality, by every available measurement and by simple observation, has sagged, not least in the public and high schools. The Canadian Test of Basic Skills, designed to measure performance in language skills and mathematics, has seen the composite scores of grade 8 students decline by 6.3 percent between 1966 and 1991. Similarly, in the 1930s, grade 1 students were expected to be able to read 850 different words; in the 1960s the goal was 675 words; today the expectation is 300 words, although, incredibly, between the 1960s and the 1990s, spending per student more than doubled. Further proof that money is not the solution was provided when, in 1995 and 1996, 31 percent of Alberta high school graduates proceeding to university failed their mathematics examination. In Ontario in 1968, the first year without provincewide examinations, 69 percent of students scored above 60 percent averages in grade 13; over the previous five years, 47 to 55 percent of students scored above 60 percent. Even more striking, in 1966 only 3 percent of Ontario high school students had averages above 80 percent and were awarded Ontario Scholarships. By 1992, this figure had soared to 44.3 percent. The same "upward slippage" in grades can be found in every province. In effect, either the students have become smarter or, much more likely, their

---

3. And what is a university (or an employer) to do with a school board that deliberately decides its policy is not to fail students? The Sherbrooke, Quebec, Commission des écoles catholique officially proclaims this policy, and at least one Quebec English-language board (Lakeshore) has the same attitude — unofficially. Montreal *Gazette*, 14 August 1996.

teachers have become more lenient — exactly as university professors have with their students.

No one believes that the students are better trained. An article in the *Toronto Star* of 30 October 1996 signed by twenty-two professors stated bluntly that "students are less and less able to comprehend the same books; less and less able to listen attentively...less and less aware how to prepare for an exam, write a paper, research a subject in the library." And it is not the few dullards, the professors said; "it is the majority of students."

Universities all across Canada have been forced to establish courses in remedial English or French in an effort to bring students up to the required level to cope with university. The Université du Québec à Montréal found that 65 percent of its incoming students in 1993 failed a French competency test; at Calgary in the first six years of English testing, nearly half the incoming students failed. A Calgary political scientist stated the simple truth when he noted: "We are too often getting an inferior product from the secondary school system, which means that students are too often getting short-changed." The president of McGill University's students' society in 1985 agreed: "It seems somewhat unfair for society to expect the university to fulfill a mandate that primary and secondary schools could not."

Most Canadians, scarcely believing what is occurring, do not seem to worry about declining high school standards. Foreigners, however, do. The United States Foreign Service pays for the children of its officers serving in Canada to attend private high schools, with costs per student being upwards of $10,000. Why? Canadian public high schools in most provinces have no standardized tests and, in their absence, it is difficult for their graduates to secure access to good American universities. The private schools' grades are taken more seriously. That is a stunning vote of no confidence in Canadian education. As it is, the private schools maintain that even their grades are not given full weight. Upper Canada College in Toronto, frustrated that foreign universities still compare its students with public high school graduates, is moving to the International Baccalaureate system in an attempt to ensure that its first-class applicants get admitted to the universities of their choice. Whether the private schools offer a better education is not proven, but Canadian parents, including professors, who want the best education possible for their offspring and can afford it are increasingly sending their children to private schools. It used to be an article of faith that Canadian schooling, like Canadian beer, was better than the U.S. variety. No longer.[4]

No one should be surprised that the demand for a return to provincewide examinations is mounting, despite the recognition that such examinations are expensive to administer, may be culturally and socioeconomically biased, and lead teachers to emphasize tests instead of creative thinking. Tests of student achievement, designed to measure systemwide trends rather than individual progress, are creeping back across Canada, pressed by suddenly cooperative Ministries of Education. British Columbia has standardized tests in major subjects, with the results counting substantially in grades. The largest province, Ontario, resisted tests for years, but it has now established an Education Quality and Accountability Office with the mandate to conduct provincewide tests and monitor school quality. Even better, in contrast to the multiple choice, standardized, computer-graded tests used in the other provinces that have gone this route, Ontario will make the students write. In 1994, Ontario introduced a grade 9 reading and writing test, though there were complaints that the test was very mushy and light on any requirements for knowledge. In 1997, Ontario is testing grade 3 students on reading, writing, and arithmetic; then grade 6 students; and later still grade 9 and 11 classes. This is progress, and Ontario parents may actually have reason to hope that the sliding

---

4. Journalist and teacher William Hynes argued that because the number of Canadians attending university outside the country rose from 14,132 in 1975 to 27,437 in 1995, Canadian high school standards must be good. We do not doubt that many of these expatriates are the brightest products of our school systems, but we see such numbers instead as an indicator that increasing numbers of parents and students fear that Canadian university standards have fallen. "Kudos to Our Classrooms," *Globe and Mail*, 31 August 1996.

quality of the province's schools can be slowed. That would be a giant step forward.

There are similar demands for national standards in the United States, where schools are afflicted with the same difficulties. In the United States, however, the Scholastic Aptitude Test, a requirement for university admission virtually everywhere, at least measures reasoning along with verbal and mathematical abilities, and the best schools take in the students with the highest scores, no matter what built-in biases the tests may have. Canada has no such system and, in the face of collapsing standards, no one should be surprised at the growing call for provincial or national testing. Predictably, high school teachers generally oppose such tests, and Quebec, unsurprisingly, objects to anything that smacks of federal intrusion. But high school teachers are parents too, and so are Québécois. This might be the one area where the universities and the federal government could successfully go over the head of Quebec City and the bureaucracies that control the teachers' federations in every province. In an era when Ottawa seems to be pulling out of programs, the creation and defence of Canadian educational standards could be a useful task for the federal government.

In the absence of any reliable standards, universities that retain a vestigial interest in quality predictably and quietly began to keep lists of the good and bad high schools in their "catchment areas." University X will know that High School 1 inflates its grades by 10 percent on average over those of High School 2. If it can, it will take this inflation into account in its offers of admission. If it can . . . But as we have suggested, other factors can determine the numbers allowed into the hallowed and ivy-covered halls.

There is only one conclusion that can be drawn from this discussion. The public schools and high schools have failed and continue to fail to do their job, and the universities are compounding the problem. There are too many students in the universities who should never have been admitted "either because they lacked sufficient academic skills and knowledge," Nova Scotia's 1985 Royal Commission on Post-Secondary

Education said, "or because they had a mistaken notion of the purpose of a university education and its suitability for themselves." Today's students, simply put, cannot understand the books and articles their predecessors did twenty years ago. They do not read for pleasure, they write poorly, they know no history, and while they may know how to browse the World Wide Web, computer literacy is not the same as literacy, just as following current events (which few enough do) is not the same as understanding history. There are many exceptions, to be sure, but the reality is as we state it. A university system built on the assumption that every university could offer every program and that the money would roll in forever only worsened this situation.

A decade later, Nova Scotia is tackling the problems it faces. With thirteen universities in a small province, it faced massive problems of duplication and administrative waste. Halifax's Dalhousie University is big and all the others are small, and although it stands only in the middle of *Maclean's* rankings, Dalhousie has been hated locally because of its relative size and heft. Now the Liberal government has bludgeoned Dalhousie and the six universities in the metropolitan Halifax area to form a "Metro Halifax Universities Consortium" to coordinate course offerings, the appointment of faculty, and a large and growing array of administrative functions. In time, there will be a common course calendar, and what we might call, prematurely, the "University of Nova Scotia" will have come into existence. For the first time, a Maritime university will at last be able to compete with Ontario's research-intensive schools, and if it can attract the best students in the area and first-class students from elsewhere in Canada and abroad, it has the potential to be the best university in the Atlantic region and the peer of any university in the country.

The same process, again in different ways, is happening elsewhere. Saskatchewan is beginning to contemplate merging the Universities of Saskatchewan and Regina. In British Columbia, the University of British Columbia already holds a dominant position, much like Edmonton's University of Alberta. The big are getting bigger and, maybe, better.

In Ontario, the "research intensive" universities, with professional faculties (e.g., medicine, law, engineering, dentistry) and heavy investment in PhD programs, are making the case to Queen's Park, apparently with success, that they need and deserve more money than the second-rank universities that lack their high-cost research programs and superior quality. At the same time, their university presidents are arguing that they should be able to charge whatever tuition the market will bear to their dental, medical, and business school students — and especially to Executive MBAs, which are unashamedly seen as money makers. At Queen's University in Kingston, Ontario, the ordinary MBA program already charges $22,000 a year in tuition, and the University of Western Ontario is proposing $36,000 as its MBA tuition by the year 2000. Western has also demonstrated that a dentistry student paid $3278 in tuition in 1995–96 compared with the $2620 paid by a student in social sciences. It costs $40,174 to educate that dentistry student, however, compared with $5725 for the social sciences student, a grossly inequitable situation since, as the university has said, "the graduates of Dentistry on average have much higher earning expectations than the graduates of Social Science. Why should the dental students pay such a remarkably small percentage of the costs of their education?" Why indeed? Eventually a separate — and vastly unequal — fee schedule will result among faculties. And it is only a matter of time before Toronto, Queen's, and Western demand — and secure — the right to charge all their students premium tuition fees for the privilege of attending a so-called quality university.

Ontario then will have a multi-tier system of higher education, with the research-intensive universities at the top and the community colleges at the bottom. In between will be a range of institutions: boutique universities, like the University of Waterloo with its engineering and math, and Oxford wannabes, like Peterborough's Trent; big, second-rank schools like York, serving the northern Toronto suburbs; and regional institutions, like Lakehead University in Thunder Bay, meeting the needs of far-flung parts of the province.

The one potential spanner in the works in this hypothetical Ontario restructuring is that the Harris government's Ministry of Education seems fixated on stressing teaching over research, a recipe for the destruction of the research-intensive institutions.[5] And its comments appear to support accessibility over quality every bit as much as its NDP and Liberal predecessors did. A panel on university education, created in July 1996 by the Harris government, may provide some clear indications where Ontario will go.

Still, differentiation, another of the new buzzwords of the 1990s, is in the air. What it means is clear: all universities are not alike. Some will offer different and expensive-to-mount programs; some will be better than others and recognized as such; and some will charge their students more. In effect, the universities are at last beginning to go through the process that hospitals have had forced upon them. Some big city hospitals are "full-service" institutions, offering everything from first-class surgeons doing open-heart surgery to obstetrical care and emergency wards. Others provide only ambulatory care, looking after walk-in traffic with lesser ailments. There is a qualitative difference there, of course; there is also, necessarily, a resource difference.

In the next decade, we fully expect to see the emergence of what will be recognized as "ambulatory care" universities to cater to the Canadian penchant for accessibility — every student who graduates from high school, whatever her or his grade average, Canadians have somehow come to believe, is entitled by God-given right to a place in a university somewhere. The faculty at Ambulatory Care U — schools such as Lethbridge, Laurentian, Chicoutimi, and Cape Breton — will primarily be teachers, their research interests given short shrift as they face higher teaching loads, larger classes, and receive lower salaries for their efforts at instructing the nation's multitude of less capable or less

5. The Ontario approach appears to be based on Dr Stuart Smith's *Report on Canadian University Education* (1991), which was commissioned by the Association of Universities and Colleges of Canada and might have been expected to know better. A former Ontario Liberal leader, Smith denounced the universities for devaluing teaching and allowing active researchers to teach so little. Somehow, the idea that if active researchers taught more they would do less active researching did not appear to occur to Smith, or the Ontario government.

fortunate students. At the same time, the "full-service" universities in the Canadian metropolises will attract the ablest scholars into their relatively highly paid faculty ranks and get the lion's share of provincial funding for their libraries, buildings, and courses. We also expect distance education to expand dramatically, bringing higher education to even more people and at a reasonable cost to users and institutions. All this amounts to radical change, to be sure, but it is inevitable and essential if Canada is to have any universities that can compete with the best in other countries. Today, we have none.

This process of differentiation is long overdue. No one who has taught in or attended more than one university in Canada has any illusions about the huge qualitative differences that have long existed. While there have been a number of published guides to Canadian universities, *Maclean's* was the first to point the finger in public in a major way, and all credit to its editors. No one was surprised at the universities that were at the bottom of the list — except perhaps students and the university administrators who had gulled their provincial governments into financing their campuses at the same per-student level as better institutions. The earthquake has just started to rumble.

The results of these policies on higher education have been simply disastrous. Academic overexpansion promoted by a policy of accessibility and followed by government cutbacks is a particularly toxic combination. The available academic dollars have been spread thinly, so thinly that the holes are showing in the post-secondary facade. There are still pockets of excellence, still good faculty and good students. But the system is frayed, the faculty are increasingly cynical and discouraged, and the students will again be the victims of the latest fads in social engineering. Other countries have no problem in maintaining their élite schools, whether publicly financed or as private institutions, to cater to their brightest; in Canada, out of a misguided sense of anti-élitism and a naive belief that accessibility will cure all problems, we have succeeded in turning gold into dross.

The problem is not entirely the universities' fault. Canadians have often confused size and space. We have space aplenty, but in size of population Canada ranks behind Spain, Poland, and Romania and, for that matter, California. Our resources are spread too thin. This, we realize, is partly the result of the Canadian talent for infinite constitutional subdivision, our habit of erecting imaginary fences around real problems.

What Canada needs is a small number of first-class universities that will cater to the best students, attract the ablest faculty, and receive greater government funding than the lower-quality universities. Canadians still have the resources to turn the Universities of British Columbia, Alberta, Western Ontario, Toronto, Queen's, Montreal, and Dalhousie, for example, into such schools — if only they recognize the reality that other schools will not, and can not, be of equal quality, except in some specialized areas. Instead of pretending that University A is equal to University Z, we should accept that some schools will be first rate, some will be specialist institutions, and some will exist to serve regional needs or lesser-quality students. That would serve excellence *and* accessibility in a way that Canada's higher education does not presently do.

It would also be useful if Canada had a few private universities, institutions that took nothing from government (other than research grants won in open competition) and charged whatever they could induce students to pay. The Ontario Tory government has made a few ideologically inspired noises that suggest it is thinking along these lines and in favour of self-funded programs, but the conversion of a public institution into a private one would be difficult indeed; the start-up costs to create a new private university are obviously enormous for buildings, libraries, laboratories, and computers, although there may be possible savings in using extensively the new world of virtual reality. In Victoria, British Columbia, the old Royal Roads Military College, shut down by the federal government in its fit of post–Cold War defence budget downsizing, has been turned into a private university. Charging high fees, using adjunct and visiting faculty heavily, the new Royal Roads University intends to turn itself into a small and élite institution. If it succeeds — and the odds are against it — the idea of private universities may take on some renewed life in Canada.

Such a heretical idea predictably stirs up the egalitarians. Private universities will create a two-tier system, they say. But Canada already has qualitatively different universities, as *Maclean's* annual surveys have demonstrated. Does anyone except the incurably naive or the wilfully blind truly believe that all Canada's universities are equal? They never have been and they certainly are not in the late 1990s. We see nothing whatsoever wrong with private universities — some competition for the publicly supported system could only be a good thing.

Some will argue that we are élitists who want to keep women, people of colour, and the poor out of higher education. To these critics, accessibility is no threat to quality and, even if it were, then accessibility should prevail. Very simply, this is nonsense. In the first place, women already outnumber male students at the universities and have done so since the early 1980s; the present ratio is four to three. Second, we cheerfully admit to being élitists if that means we accept that talents are distributed unequally, that most will be followers and few leaders. But we refuse to believe that women, people of colour, and the poor are any less bright on average than white middle-class males or that the percentage of truly gifted is less among the economically disadvantaged. We refuse to believe that the ablest in the hitherto disadvantaged groups in society are foolish enough to want — or to accept — a third-rate education as their due. We believe that Canada must give the highest-quality education it can provide to everyone who is capable of benefiting from it, something we now notably fail to do. If this means a university system that recognizes the reality that all universities, like all students, are not the same, it is already long past time for us to do so.

We believe that Canada is rich enough to have at least one national university that is demonstrably first rate. Such an institution, bilingual and well-funded by the federal and provincial governments, could be the finest university in the country. Open to the best students, the national university could demonstrate that education is valued in Canada. What a change that would be!

Chapter 4

Planning for the Future:
New Challenges and Honoured Traditions

ONCE CANADIAN UNIVERSITY CAMPUSES were places where professors professed, students studied, and administrators provided the shelter, heat, and plumbing so those other two activities could happen in one place. These days it seems as if planning, not teaching and learning, is the most pervasive activity on university campuses. Across Canada, millions of pages of plans, forecasts, vision statements, and goals and strategies documents are being written, photocopied, stapled, bound, delivered, debated, and then decried or embraced. Canadian universities have declared war on chaos and have taken up the apparent order of planning. Few of the new converts to planning seem to have discovered what German general Helmuth von Moltke declared long ago: "No plan survives first contact with the enemy."

There is without doubt more of this planning going on inside the halls of Canadian academe today than in the entire history of higher education in this country. The universities of Canada are looking at themselves with a critical eye, trying to evaluate what they have been doing over the past quarter century and trying to decide what they ought to be doing in the next quarter century. Some are aiming at nothing less than wholesale reconstruction, changing the way they teach, changing what they teach, and challenging the very basic assumptions of what a university education is. They are trying to discern what they can do to remain relevant and competitive in a time of rapidly shifting public financing priorities, new technologies, and a growing divergence of public expectations.

The list of planning-obsessed institutions is long.[1] Within these universities, a tremendously broad range of planning initiatives are now under way. Acadia University, for example, is a small liberal arts institution located in Wolfville, Nova Scotia. In March 1996 the university announced "The Acadia Advantage" — a plan to make Acadia Canada's first liberal arts institution with a completely electronic campus. Its classrooms, laboratories, residences, and offices will be equipped with the latest in communications technology. All entering students will eventually be provided with laptop computers. Faculty will be trained or retrained in the use of advanced educational technologies. All this will be accomplished with the help of strategic partnerships with corporations such as IBM Canada and American Express. Each student who entered Acadia's computer science and business administration programs in September 1996 was issued the latest IBM ThinkPad computer.

In the fall of 1995 McGill University's senate and board of governors launched its planning exercise by considering a document entitled "Towards a New McGill," prepared and distributed by Principal Bernard Shapiro. The document laid out a broad range of issues to be examined in developing a new future for McGill, and a task force was established to study some of those considerations. It concluded that shifting student demographics pose a significant challenge to McGill; that problems caused by government cutbacks and a high debt load demand immediate attention; that the university as currently

---

1. The list includes Acadia University, Athabasca University, Carleton University, Concordia University, McGill University, McMaster University, Mount Saint Vincent University, Queen's University, Simon Fraser University, University of Alberta, University of Calgary, University of Guelph, University of Lethbridge, University of Manitoba, University of New Brunswick, University of Northern British Columbia, University of Ottawa, University of Saskatchewan, University of Toronto, University of Victoria, University of Waterloo, University of Western Ontario, and York University.

structured badly needs to reassess its ability to meet the growing demand for interdisciplinary research and learning; and that the university's biggest single task is to overcome low staff morale. In partial response to these challenges, McGill announced in the spring of 1996 that it will privatize some of its graduate degree programs, starting with those in business.

Queen's University, another of Canada's "ivy league" institutions, has been deeply involved in planning since 1992, when the Principal's Advisory Task Force on Resource Issues was established. Queen's is studying a wide range of issues in its search to prepare for new times and changing trends. Among these issues are a desire to provide a greatly enhanced international learning environment; a teaching and learning environment conducive to interdisciplinary studies; and a financial structure that can deal effectively with declining government support by increasing other forms of revenue and by using the university's own economic resources to help fund itself.

Fully cognizant that budget cuts will inevitably lead to more tuition increases, Queen's plans to use an increasing share of its revenues to provide flexible student aid packages. It is also aware that higher fees will mean greater expectations among its students and a lower tolerance for substandard teaching and research programs. To that end, Queen's plans to increase the rigour of its ongoing evaluation of departments, schools, and faculties and to link that evaluation system with the university's decision-making process.

At the University of Calgary, a Coordination Task Force was established in the spring of 1996 with no less a mission than to define a new future for the university. After evaluating staff and student concerns, the CTF challenged the university to choose among five different futures, ranging from concentration on undergraduate liberal arts education to the establishment of a research-intensive university not unlike that of California's Stanford University.

At the University of Victoria, a Strategic Planning Task Force was set up in 1994 at the direction of the university senate and board of governors. It was charged with the task of looking a decade ahead to identify choices and to make recommendations for the university to follow. The key recommendations to date state that the university's undergraduate program should be more focused, more current, and more coherent; the graduate student component should be raised to 15 percent of total enrolment; new research centres and institutes should promote multidisciplined research; and a commitment to environmental responsibility should be carried through in the university's teaching, curriculum research, and operational activities.

———————

The current planning mania grows directly from the turmoil and uncertainty that is now affecting virtually every university in Canada and, indeed, in the developed world. Government cutbacks, technological change, competition from other forms of post-secondary education, rising public expectations, and increased demands for public accountability are all having an impact. Indeed, some specialists in the history of higher education believe that today's universities are entering a period of transformation as momentous as that which occurred some five hundred years ago when Europe's major universities began to split away from the Roman Catholic Church.

The current period of transformation, we are told, will see great changes in virtually everything the universities do and will be predicated on the widespread distribution of knowledge via new technologies. The new prophecies of higher education vary both in tone and in the content of their message, but they speak to a single underlying theme: when people can plug into the World Wide Web and learn virtually everything their hearts desire, there will be no place left for universities as we have known them for the past thousand years.

In fact, it is too early to say whether a period of truly revolutionary change is in the offing for universities in Canada and abroad. It is always difficult for anyone living at the dawn of a new age to see the larger picture and to determine the long-term patterns in it. Almost no one living in Britain in the latter decades of the eighteenth century, for example, would have thought of the period as the "Industrial Revolution." Reading broad trends in history is not unlike trying to describe an entire forest after studying a few stands of trees.

Great change in universities has been trumpeted continually since the early 1960s at least, but almost none of the major transformations forecast then actually came about. The stark evidence of the failure of the forecasters is attached to the walls of many lecture halls built in Canada in the 1960s — brackets that once held the monstrous TV sets that were supposed to replace live lecturers. For the most part, it never happened.

But something does seem to be happening now. The introduction of truly new and widely available dissemination technologies may eventually prove as momentous for universities in Canada and around the world as the steam engine did for manufacturing at the dawn of the Industrial Revolution. In fact, there is a parallel between current trends in higher education in Canada and elsewhere and what happened to manufacturing, beginning in the mid-1700s.

Every schoolchild is taught that the Industrial Revolution came about when steam power was harnessed to do work previously carried out by humans, animals, or natural elements such as wind or water. Patented in England by James Watt in 1769, the steam engine provided power for the machines that made the Industrial Revolution possible. The essence of that revolution was the concentration of manufacturing in one place — the factory. Prior to that, entrepreneurs collected raw materials in whatever way they could, brought those materials to the homes and tiny shops of skilled workers, then collected the finished products and brought them to market.

Steam-powered machines and steam-powered transportation revolutionized that process; henceforth, raw materials and workers were brought together in the factory, where centralized production was organized. This centralization allowed manufacturers to further refine the productive process in the mid to late nineteenth century through, for example, assembly-line production, standardized parts, and time and motion techniques. It also allowed manufacturers to link factories

together by rail or by water, so that all (or virtually all) of the productive process, from the extraction of raw material to the sale of the
finished product to the consumer, was controlled by a single enterprise.
In this way the great monopolies, trusts, and cartels began which dominated American and Canadian capitalism at the beginning of the
twentieth century.

In a way, universities had the process of concentration in place at
least eight hundred years before the manufacturers. The great early
universities of Bologna and Paris were begun by students who banded
together to hire teachers. They wanted to learn whatever there was to
know, hence the word *universitas*. Within the larger university community, particular groups of students who wished to specialize in some
specific type of knowledge formed colleges. That was the origin of
today's self-governing, professional colleges such as the Royal College
of Physicians and Surgeons of Canada. At these early universities, students learned by attending lectures or by taking part in discussion
groups presided over by their teachers. When the universities began to
build up collections of books and manuscripts, the union of libraries and
universities took place and the earliest research institutions emerged.

Universities concentrated most of what was required for advanced
learning in one place — the campus. The students came to where the
professors were (or vice versa) and the libraries were established there
to aid the process of teaching and learning. The laboratories which first
demonstrated the arts of alchemy, or which contained the astronomical
instruments used to cast horoscopes, were later built or acquired for the
same purposes as the libraries — to aid learning. Everything that the
students and the professors needed to learn and to teach was available
in one convenient location.

The modern university is a product of that centralizing process.
Today's research-intensive universities house libraries with literally
millions of volumes of books, periodicals, and other knowledge "packages" in every conceivable media, from aural tapes and microfiche to
CD-ROMs. They also house specialized laboratories costing millions of
dollars which are dedicated to the particular pursuit of different areas

of the natural, physical, or social sciences. A mechanical engineering laboratory and a microbiology laboratory, for example, are different in both layout and equipment, and very different from a cognitive psychology laboratory.

———————

The Second World War marked the beginning of the end of two centuries of factory-centred manufacturing. The earth satellite and the electronic computer, both direct outcomes of improvements in military technology, gave entrepreneurs the world over the means to undo the centralization of the Industrial Revolution. It is now possible for a manufacturing enterprise to communicate instantly with suppliers, branch-plants, and marketers around the globe by voice, television, or data uplink. The new modes of communication allow corporations to spin off or "outsource" those portions of their manufacturing processes that are more economically done elsewhere. A car manufacturer in, say, Oshawa, Ontario, may decide that certain engine parts should be made in an Asian country, while certain electronic parts should be made in a Latin American country. The reasons will vary — cheaper labour, higher productivity, better climate, greater social stability, or being closer to raw materials — but the motive is always the same. Why make something in Oshawa that someone else can make more cheaply and more efficiently in another place?

Sometimes much or even most of the spinoff is done within one company — a major computer manufacturer based in the United States may decide to build its own monitors in a wholly owned assembly plant in Mexico. Planning, production, and shipping of those monitors are coordinated via the company's own global communications links. Alternatively, that same company may "outsource" by ceasing to produce monitors and by contracting to buy those made by another company. The old seamless production links that ran from the sources of raw material, through the factories, to the consumer outlets are being chopped into their basic parts. What once had to be done in one widget factory, or factory complex, can now be done at a dozen or more subsidiary plants or outsourced locations around the globe, then brought together for final assembly.

The same technological advances that have undermined factory-centred manufacturing are now threatening campus-centred learning. In some university disciplines it is no longer necessary for students, scholars, and libraries to be gathered in one place. The process is not unlike developments taking place in the world of manufacturing, but this time the universities are lagging behind the newest trends, not leading them.

What are the new technologies available to universities, to teachers, and to students? They are essentially of two types — real time and shift time. Real-time technologies allow students and teachers to communicate over long distances almost as if they were in the same room at the same time. The best but most expensive of these technologies is video conferencing over land lines or by satellite uplink. Audio links, such as those used in teleconferencing, are considerably cheaper. Net-links, using the Internet, are the cheapest of these new technologies. They can deliver information via standard mouse or keyboard inputs, aural hardware, even baseball-sized video cameras. But they depend on up-to-date hardware and software, and connections can be difficult to establish at heavy demand periods. Some Canadian distance education programs provide the necessary equipment and add the cost to the total program tuition fee.

Shift-time devices store information that students can use more or less at their convenience. The primary means are aural and video tapes, with printed materials and visual aids such as maps, photographs, and slides. These sources are usually packaged in course kits. Students using this method to learn are almost always given access by telephone to tutors at prearranged hours or are invited to periodic lectures or seminars near where they live. These shift-time methods of learning and instruction have been around for some time and are still widely used in so-called correspondence courses.

Though they are tried and true, the pure correspondence method of course delivery (normally by mail) is hugely wasteful. Attrition rates average well over 75 percent, no doubt because student contact with instructors is infrequent and because the students study for the most part at their own pace. Programs and courses delivered by the new, real-time technologies are vastly different. They are timetabled and taught as any course on campus would be. Deadlines for term work are similar, and mid-term exams and final exams are scheduled as they would be on campus. Students are expected to work at a predetermined pace and are in frequent and regular contact with their teachers or seminar leaders, though they obviously cannot wander at will into their offices.

When we write about new technologies for distance learning, we are *not* talking about "surfing the net" or "plugging into the Web." Much of the information that is simply "out there" on the Web is pure glitz and is of no use whatever to a student seeking to learn how to learn, as in a university. It is not possible yet, in our view, for someone sitting at a computer for forty-eight months (or any number of months) of unstructured, though diligent, searching of the Web to experience anything remotely resembling a university education. But those traditionalists in universities who dismiss modern distance education as just "surfing the net" are ignoring the very real possibilities that now exist for learning enhancement through new technologies. They are also ignoring the serious challenges these new technologies are posing to the traditional university.

———————

In some ways, this challenge couldn't have come at a worse time. Government funding of universities has declined drastically in Canada over the last half-decade as both federal and provincial governments cut their budgets to get runaway deficits and debt under control. Although the rate and the size of the cuts have varied across Canada, they have been deep almost everywhere. Alberta affords the best example. When the Conservative government of Premier Ralph Klein was returned to office in the spring of 1993, Alberta had one of the highest per capita debts in Canada. The solution was obvious: immediate and deep cuts in provincial expenditures. The province's universities were to lose 21 percent of their direct provincial grants over three years; 4 percent of that was to be returned to them (and to other institutions of advanced learning in the province) through competitive applications to a new Access Fund.

The cuts came at a time when the demand for spaces in Alberta's universities was skyrocketing, partially because of expansion in the population but more particularly because of growing participation among adult learners. Some of the cuts would be recovered through higher tuition fees; the government allowed universities to raise most tuition fees to a higher ceiling and at a faster pace. But the government did not deregulate tuition fees, as some university officials and faculty demanded.

Not long after the Alberta cuts were instituted, Ottawa announced major cuts in transfer payments to provinces as part of its debt-fighting plan. The Alberta government apparently judged that the cuts it was forcing on its own advanced education sector were deep enough and decided not to pass these federal transfer payment cuts on to its universities and colleges. (It was running a surplus of almost a billion dollars at the time.) But other federal cost-saving measures had an impact on the Alberta scene anyway. The budgets of the major national granting agencies — the Social Sciences and Humanities Research Council, the Natural Sciences and Enginering Research Council, and the Medical Research Council — were slashed. These cuts reduced grant funds awarded to individual university researchers and to graduate students in Alberta and elsewhere in Canada.

There was really only one way that Alberta's universities could meet their budget reduction targets, since they are not, by law, allowed to use deficit financing. They had to make deep cuts in salary and compensation as quickly as possible. Salaries of support staff, professors, technical personnel, and teaching assistants normally make up more than 80 percent of any university's budget. So, people had to go. They went mainly through early retirement incentives. Very few of them were replaced. Some of those who went were among Alberta's better researchers, and their departure cut into their university's grant and contract revenues.

Budget cuts, shrinking staff, growing demand, and increased tuition fees are now the rule in Alberta. The equation is the same across the country, although the numbers differ from province to province and even from university to university within provinces. The impact on the attitude of students and the larger community has also been similar; students demand more quality, as they should, in return for higher fees, while the community worries that accessibility will suffer. There are renewed complaints from the business and corporate community, first heard loudly in the late 1970s, that universities are not responsive, or are largely irrelevant, or do not teach "important" things that graduates can use when they go to work in the business and corporate sector. Provincial governments seem much more sensitive to these matters today than ever. In Alberta a complex index of performance has been created by the Department of Advanced Education and Career Development in consultation with the province's universities and colleges. It will measure factors such as percentage of graduates who enter the workforce in appropriate jobs, attrition rates, and revenue generation. In future, part of the province's grant to Alberta universities and colleges will be based on how well they perform according to these measurements.

It is these main factors — budget cuts, demands for greater accessibility, public scrutiny, the search for relevance — that is driving virtually all the planning that is going on in Canadian universities today. In one way the explanation is very simple: universities are thrashing about trying to discover how to do a better job with less government-sourced resources. The new environment gives them little option but to begin to search their souls and to ask fundamental questions about what and who they are, and where they are going. The planners need to remember, however, that planning is not an end in itself and that the solutions they spin must reflect not only the opportunities that new technologies offer but also the basic university mission of promoting individual self-awareness.

————————

Canada's traditional universities face stiff competition these days. Much of that competition comes from other forms of post-secondary education or from other universities. Virtually all Canadian universities engage in some form of advertisement or recruitment for both graduate and undergraduate students. In itself that is not new. What is new — and novel — is the intensification and the reach of this recruitment. It has become a matter of course for universities in one city or province to advertise themselves in other cities and provinces. The advertising is done in newspapers and magazines — and not only in "special" editions devoted to post-secondary education. It is done through the establishment of home pages on the Web and through direct mail aimed at targeted markets.

In part, this advertising is intended to help universities in regions of flat or declining undergraduate enrolment to keep their numbers up. But it is also intended to attract graduate students whose presence is vital for institutions with heavy research programs. Although research in the humanities, social sciences, and fine arts still tends to be centred on the lone researcher, research in the hard sciences is almost always a team effort directed by the senior researcher/faculty member and consisting of several graduate students working on their own theses, as well as a technician or two. Take away the graduate students, and the research cannot be done. There are more than enough applications for seats in Canadian graduate schools today to fill all available spaces, but there are not nearly enough applications from top-ranked Canadian-born or landed immigrant undergraduates. Much of the recruiting of graduate students in Canada is aimed at that relatively small group and at top-ranked international students.

Graduate enrolments and job demands are rarely in sync with each other. Recruiting is vital in areas such as engineering, where relatively few graduates want to go on to do research degrees, but it is totally unnecessary in large areas of the social science and humanities, where graduate degrees qualify their holders for little other than university teaching. In the United States a growing percentage of PhDs in the sciences enter industry right out of graduate school, with no intention of teaching in universities. Little research has been done on this phenomenon in Canada, but anecdotal evidence points in the same direction. Such is not the case, and will probably never be the case, with holders of PhDs in history or English, for example. In the former discipline there were well over one hundred students working towards PhDs in history at the University of Toronto alone in 1996, yet there were no more than a dozen tenure-track history jobs in all of Canada. There are approximately 800 students pursuing PhDs in English in Canada today, but there were only forty-one entry level positions in English at all Canadian universities in 1995. In other words, among these graduate students, roughly one in twenty will get the jobs they seek. Why are all those people in graduate school? If they are there to satisfy their curiosity, get a broader education, or delay their entry into the job market, well and good. But many will end up in one-year sessional appointments, moving from city to city, providing university administrators with low-wage alternatives to full-fledged tenure-track appointments. That will continue as long as tenure continues.

What, then, is the responsibility of universities towards potential graduate students? This is a free country and people must have the right to choose career paths, even in the full knowledge that chances for regular employment are slim. But do they have that knowledge? If they do, it is not because universities are providing it. Many departments across Canada try to apprise applicants in some way about the job market in their discipline, but there is virtually no concerted effort by any of the learned societies, by the Association of Universities and Colleges of Canada, by the Canadian Association of University Teachers, or by governments to let potential graduate students know just what their chances are of finding steady employment in their chosen field. With today's scarcity of advanced education resources, that is simply irresponsible. It is only a matter of time before governments set their own

quotas on how many students will be allowed into which graduate programs, since vast sums are wasted on educating PhD holders who cannot find work in their chosen fields. It would be far better if the
educational establishment took action on its own.

Canadian universities are also in direct competition with universities in the United States (and some other foreign countries) in providing a wide range of professional certification degrees such as the Master
of Education (MEd) and Master of Business Administration (MBA). In
western Canada, for example, there were at least nine such U.S. institutions offering graduate degrees in the spring of 1996. These degrees
ranged from PhDs in psychology, offered by the Fielding Institute, to
the MEd, offered by the University of Portland.

One of the pioneers of these distance education degrees, and currently one of the largest in terms of enrolment, is Nova Southeastern
University, based in Fort Lauderdale, Florida. Nova has a total enrolment on and off campus of more than 12,000 students. The majority
take their degrees in distance education programs such as the Doctor of
Education (EdD) and the MBA. Nova lays out the curriculum, contracts
for local classrooms and library resources, provides locally hired tutors
or lecturers, and organizes major lectures by visiting high-profile faculty
or via video conferencing. The fees are high and generate handsome
revenues for the university. There is a vast market for such distance
graduate education, particularly in small centres far from universities
or among people employed full time who cannot hope to meet the strict
residence requirements of almost all Canadian graduate schools.

Nova is only one of dozens of U.S. institutions that are deeply
engaged in real-time distance education. The Education Network of
Maine televises college and university courses throughout the state.
Syracuse University mounts a full Master of Library Science over the
Internet. The privately owned University of Phoenix (a profit-making
institution whose shares are traded on the stock market) offers a full
list of degree programs via the Internet. These U.S.-based distance
education graduate programs vary in quality, but so do Canadian graduate programs.

Until very recently, U.S.-based distance education institutions enjoyed some distinct advantages over Canadian universities. The U.S. universities, being outside provincial regulation, were able to charge whatever they desired for their programs of study. Most provincial governments exercise strict control over fees and prohibit their own universities from charging differential fees that might cover the costs of delivering distance education programs. So, for example, the University of Calgary could not charge a higher fee to deliver an MEd in Fort McMurray, Alberta, than it could on the Calgary campus. In effect, that restriction meant that the university could run a distance education program only at a loss, something it could not afford to do.

The greatest advantage the out-of-country universities enjoyed, however, was that most Canadian universities recoiled at the very thought that distance-delivered programs were legitimate. This attitude is still dominant in Canadian universities. They tend to place as much emphasis on the process by which a graduate student gains a degree as they do on the research generated in the form of a thesis or dissertation. A student working towards an MSc in almost all Canadian universities is usually required to spend up to a year "in residence" — which loosely means on campus. Generally, an MSc student will take courses or do experimental work for all or part of that residence period, but not necessarily. How many courses is usually determined by the department of study. Although requirements for an MSc vary from campus to campus across Canada, it does not usually matter to a graduate faculty or school exactly *what* that student does for a year, as long as it is done on campus, thus fulfilling the residency requirement. During that period, the student must pay full fees. Because U.S.-based distance education programs rarely have this residence requirement, they are not thought of by most Canadian universities as legitimate. But surely what matters in a graduate program is the quality of the research, thesis, or dissertation that the student produces. Someone who aspires to a PhD, for example, will either produce a piece of original research that adds new knowledge to human experience — and thus be qualified to hold a PhD and to be called Doctor —

or will not. Put simply, residence requirements in their present form are outdated.

Some old ways *are* slowly changing in Canada. Canadian universities are beginning to offer distance education programs, especially in fields they think will generate immense new revenues. Probably the best example is the "Executive MBA," a supposed graduate degree equivalent to the regular MBA but offered in ways intended to fit the busy schedules of corporate executives. Queen's University and the University of Western Ontario have been the most aggressive in marketing these distance education EMBAs in Canada. Charging fees in excess of $15,000 per semester, they advertise widely in daily newspapers, business publications, and direct-mail campaigns. They mount these programs in designated centres across Canada in the manner pioneered by Nova Southeastern. They have forced other universities to enter the EMBA field out of sheer self-defence.

For the most part, the EMBA is a good example of invention becoming the mother of necessity. The degree exists, therefore many corporate executives decide they must have it. The EMBA course of study in no way resembles a research program. It is the content of the program that matters, not the process of learning how to learn, which is at the heart of a traditional graduate research degree. Do all these generally successful executives really need more book-learning to become even more successful? The last time we looked, Conrad Black did not think an EMBA vital to his future success. Conrad Black, we should note, does hold a graduate degree — an MA (a research degree) in history from McGill University.

Canada's universities — indeed, those of much of the world — face three major challenges today: how to reach more "customers"; how to ensure that universities continue to "add value" to their product; and how to keep costs as low as possible in the face of declining revenues and growing resistance to major fee increases. To quote a recent report on these challenges prepared for the Organization for Economic Cooperation and Development (OECD):

> Can high-quality courses of study be offered at reasonable costs for large numbers of adults if one adds a few "innovative" programmes to otherwise unchanged institutions, perhaps while eliminating or expanding a few existing programmes? If the answer to the above question is "no" and it is necessary to take a deeper and more searching look at the assumptions that govern today's system of post-secondary education, are there lessons that the best campuses can teach distance and open learning programmes? Are there lessons that the best open and distance learning programmes can teach campuses? Will it be necessary to leave traditional definitions such as "campus," "distance" and "open learning" behind and restructure post-secondary education?

As always, the answers to complex questions are never simple. The answer to this question, and to many of the others that universities are asking themselves today, is that some things universities do must ever remain more or less as they are, but that others must change dramatically and drastically in the coming decade. Which is which?

Much of the challenge universities face today comes from the needs of what was once termed "non-traditional" learners. In past and simpler times, Canadian universities served one basic clientele — high school graduates who went on to university to gain their baccalaureates, some of whom then stayed to earn graduate degrees. There was always a certain demand for a university education from men and women in mid-career who wanted to upgrade their education but who could not afford to leave work, but few Canadian universities were prepared to meet that demand in other than token ways. One of the very few exceptions was Sir George Williams University, now part of Montreal's Concordia University, an institution that grew out of high school and university extension programs offered in the downtown area by the Young Men's Christian Association after the late 1930s.

Chartered as a full-fledged university in the 1960s, Sir George mounted full "evening" programs leading to the BA, BSc, and BComm. For a time in the mid-1960s there were more "evening" students at Sir George than there were "traditional" day students. The night program of study was laid out in such a way that a working student could take five full courses in a twelve-month period — three in the fall and winter and two in the summer — and graduate in the same four years as a day student. That was only possible because Sir George mounted a full night program that was equal in content to the day program. York University's Atkinson College was founded in the 1960s with similar aims. Until very recently, few other Canadian universities cared much about the needs of non-traditional students. They offered only a few night courses and made it virtually impossible for a person employed full time to earn a university degree in less than a very long time span, if at all.

Today's universities are called upon to serve at least four basic client groups:

- High school graduates who want to enter the world of advanced research, whether as university teachers and researchers or as researchers or research team leaders in industry.
- Men and women in mid-career who develop a desire to contribute to the advancement of knowledge in some area of research and who therefore decide to change career paths.
- High school graduates who continue on to university primarily to gain a professional accreditation degree and enter the job market without delay.
- Men and women in mid-career who want to upgrade their professional qualifications in order to advance more rapidly up the promotional ladder.

The needs of all these client groups are completely justified, but in the past Canadian universities were, on the whole, reluctant to admit that the third and fourth groups were as important as the first, except for those who wanted to be physicians, lawyers, or dentists, or that they had different but legitimate needs.

The traditional campus-centred university is going to be the locus for most students of the first two client groups for a long time to come. That is because most forms of research, particularly but not exclusively in the sciences, will continue to be based on laboratory and experimental work. Any such research will continue to require expensive equipment, operating in laboratories, and maintained by highly specialized technicians. Close teamwork is also a prerequisite of much of this sort of learning, particularly for graduate students whose own research will form part of a larger project spearheaded by the graduate supervisor.

At present, it is highly unlikely that a student interested in majoring in microbiology — a discipline based on the classic scientific method of theorizing, followed by experimentation, followed by generalization — will be able to do so anywhere other than on a university campus. This centralization is also true for students pursuing graduate degrees and for those in social sciences such as geography, psychology, archeology, and other "near" sciences.

The development of "real-time" methods of distance communication, however, means that much of the requirement for the old-fashioned style of face-to-face learning will disappear for students in some of the social science disciplines and much of the humanities. It is already possible for a history professor to lecture to and to grade an entire class that she never sees. It is even possible for her to lead a seminar of real students she will never be closer to than several hundred kilometres.

It is possible, but is it desirable? If cost effectiveness is factored out — as it surely will be when the technologies of real-time distance education become more available and thus cheaper — desirability becomes the key question. The answer will be found somewhere in a range of tradeoffs. A student on campus is able to meet and interact regularly and informally with other students and with professors. A distance education student cannot do so even through real-time "electronic" seminars. The spontaneity of contact that occurs on campus cannot be replicated by distance education techniques. But if a student in a remote location must make a choice between no university education at all and one carried out in the more formalized, regularized, impersonal atmosphere of a distance education program, the latter will win almost every time. That is especially true of students in the third and fourth client groups mentioned above.

The solution to the challenge enumerated by the OECD is not, therefore, an "either/or" one. New technologies do make it possible for many who aspire to a university education to learn off campus, especially those whose chief interests are professional accreditation or the acquisition of a body of specialized knowledge. Those Canadian universities that have long realized this dimension are on the right track. More must follow. If they do not, they will lose those increasingly important client groups who desire such an education.

A major obstacle that few institutions dedicated to distance education have been able to overcome is that the best university teachers are invariably the best researchers. They are the ones whose own research pursuits enrich their lectures and whose students — from first-year to graduate students — learn the results of their cutting-edge research long before it gets put into textbooks, or even on the Internet. Is such high-quality teaching possible in institutions that, for all intents and purposes, eschew research? Aren't most of today's dedicated distance education institutions little more than electronic junior colleges?

Sadly, the answer is yes. And thereby lies the most significant problem facing Canadian universities today. There is a growing demand for off-campus education, a demand that cannot be ignored. But most Canadian universities still mistrust distance education and relegate it to expensive and highly specialized programs such as the EMBA or the University of Calgary's Master of Distance Education degree. Nothing like the gamut of basic liberal arts education programs available at all of Canada's research universities are within reach of distance education learners. The distance education job is largely being left to "open learn-ing" institutions such as British Columbia's Open Learning Agency or dedicated distance education universities such as Athabaska University in Alberta. Some of these institutions may fancy themselves as "research" universities, but although a number of their faculty mem-bers most certainly do research and publish, such claims simply don't stand serious scrutiny.

Canada's major research universities must recognize that their mandate now includes distance education, and not just on a token scale. Curricula should be reviewed with an eye to discerning what courses, programs of study, majors and honours programs, even graduate work can be offered at a distance and particularly via real-time deliv-ery methods. Once that is done, the equipment must be acquired and the programs launched without delay. To do this will not jeopardize the primary mission of universities — to teach people how to think. In fact, it will enable universities to reach a wider audience, one that is as deserving of their attention as those able to partake of campus-centred learning.

The first primitive tools of wood, stone, and bone were nothing more than an extension of humankind's hands, feet, and brains. The computers, satellites, and jet aircraft of today are but logical extensions of those early tools. When harnessed to the mission of advanced educa-tion, new technologies can extend the reach and the sweep of higher education in Canada. The trick is to use these new technologies to enhance the basic mission of teaching people how to think, not to replace that mission.

Canada's universities are at a crossroads today. They will either learn how to adapt to new times while preserving their ancient herit-age or they will abandon their true vocation in search of perfecting the art of administration and the use of new delivery techniques. The next decade will tell the tale. The most serious obstacle that Canada's university system must overcome in the challenge to maintain time-honoured traditions while adapting to new times is the system's own shop-worn notions about what post-secondary education is today.

Chapter 5

Separating the Sheep from the Goats: Politically Incorrect Thoughts

IN THE SUMMER AND FALL OF 1995 the University of British Columbia was in turmoil. A handful of graduate students in political science had accused their professors of sexual harassment, racial prejudice, incompetent teaching, and bias of all kinds. A hugely expensive report, prepared by a Vancouver lawyer, appeared to lend credence to these claims, and the university administration, fully aware that a New Democratic Party government was in power in Victoria, hurried to act to punish the "guilty" department. Graduate admissions were stopped until such time as the Department of Political Science was cleansed. Within a few days, the media across the country were treating the UBC events as a major news story. Academic organizations and prominent individuals, male and female, were either shouting their support for the administration's actions or denouncing them. The UBC crisis escalated into a huge struggle over the corpse of the Department of Political Science.

In the midst of the crisis, when one of UBC's most distinguished political scientists dragged himself home at 10 p.m. after one more appalling day of frustration and fighting, he found himself filled with a sense of foreboding when the telephone rang. "Good Lord, what can it be now?" he thought. The sense of totalitarian dread was all-pervasive at UBC in 1995.

There once was a time when the initials *PC* were generally taken to mean Progressive Conservative or possibly privy councillor. That changed in the 1990s. Thanks to Brian Mulroney, the Progressive Conservatives entered a period — possibly a very long period — of eclipse. Privy councillors (mostly ex-Cabinet ministers) still abound, but pass unrecognized in a democratic population. However, the abbreviation *PC* is still very much with us.

PC, a term imported from the United States, now stands for "politically correct." Those who are politically correct believe in something called political correctness, and they practise, or attempt to practise, political correction on those they perceive to be their opponents. In the last few years in Canada, political correction has been much in vogue.[1] Its characteristics include, but are not limited to, the following:

- preferential hiring (usually called employment equity or affirmative action) for faculty determined by gender, race, and ethnicity;
- punitive codes restricting "offensive" or "insensitive" actions or speech, and calls for "zero tolerance" against such actions or speech on the part of faculty and students;
- the establishment of special administrators, offices, and resources to serve as representatives for and of selected student/faculty groups;
- calls for "sensitivity training" for faculty, students, and staff;
- rooting out of academic texts with so-called gender or racial bias and the adoption of inclusive language, as well as an

---

1. In their edited volume, *Beyond Political Correctness: Toward the Inclusive University* (Toronto 1995), Stephen Richer and Lorna Weir refer to *The Great Brain Robbery* as a "conservative text" concerned with the "purported" decline in the quality of higher education. Such criticism is all old hat, but then they add that our book lacked "many of the distinctive offensive moves [sic] of PC discourse, which specialize in attacks on employment equity; selective recruitment of students from social groups that have suffered systemic discrimination...and anti-sexist and anti-racist policies." We plead guilty to this sin of omission, but only because political correctness scarcely existed in 1984.

insistence on devaluing the Western canon of "great" books and ideas, and increasing study of non-Western ideas and traditions;

- demands for the "inclusive university";
- denunciation of academic freedom, as practised in the past, as designed only to support and preserve the patriarchal system that oppresses women;
- a complete lack of anything that might be called a sense of humour; and
- a sheep-like refusal to criticize the above characteristics out of a well-founded fear of retaliation.

It is undeniable that there were and there are problems of bias in Canadian universities and in Canadian society generally. Male and female professors and students have acted in sexist ways, and there have been racial insensitivities galore. Women in the past have not had their fair share of university posts and preference. The ethos of the 1950s and 1960s, especially, has hung on in Canadian universities for too many years. Academics are products of their society, and though one might expect them to be somewhat more intelligent than the norm, there is no guarantee that high intelligence translates into a greater tolerance or openness, or, for that matter, courage or independence of thought. Still, Canadian society in general is probably far more intolerant than the universities. There are biases against Caribbean and Somali blacks, East Indians, and Canadian Indians. Anti-Semitism remains powerful, and *pure laine* Québécois are quick to feel humiliated by "Anglos." In return, they discriminate, whenever they have the chance, against those Anglos who live in Quebec. Newfoundlanders are still the butt of jokes, and Hogtown is despised by every Canadian who lives beyond the boundary of Metropolitan Toronto.

Canada, in other words, is much like every other society. But Canada is different in the effort its governments and people have put into the fight against discriminatory behaviour. The Charter of Rights and Freedoms, the various provincial Human Rights codes, and a vigilant press all guarantee not that discrimination and racism will be eradicated, but that it will be exposed and challenged wherever it rears its head. This is all to the good.

But virtue often lies in its definition. In Canada, as elsewhere, the servants of virtue frequently fail to distinguish between vice and indifference. They so actively pursue evil that they abandon ordinary standards of proof, relying instead on the faith that in an imperfect (or wicked) society, evil must be everywhere. And since universities are an easy target, in part because of the conformity and timidity of their inhabitants, the vice-seekers find them a convenient hunting ground.

———

Sometimes we forget what real racism is like. One of the authors of this book went to Duke University in Durham, North Carolina, to do graduate work in 1963. The U.S. South was just then in the throes of desegregation, and Duke, a private university, reluctantly admitted its first black students that year. The school's application forms had not yet adjusted to the new realities, however, and the racial origin of the applicant had to be filled in on the appropriate line. Conscious of the equality of the races, certain of the superiority of the True North Strong and Free, the writer scrawled in "Canadian" (which is, of course, the ethnicity he still enters on Canadian census forms). Race was not a concept that Canadians considered acceptable in 1963. Within a short period, the questionnaires were revised to drop references to racial origin.

A generation later, however, the questionnaires have been revised once more, and race again is a subject of pressing interest to admissions officers. Duke University, like almost every institution in the United States, today finds itself in a near-desperate search for enough bright black students to take its scholarships and make its affirmative action programs effective. Black faculty are even more prized, and universities in the United States compete to see who can attract the few available PhDs. Canadian universities, latecomers to the search for non-white faculty, now compete in a sellers' market.

The world had changed with blinding speed, and not only in the United States. The Canadian Charter of Rights and Freedoms became law in 1982. Its section 15(1) barred "discrimination based on race, national or ethnic origin, colour, religion, sex, age or mental or physical disability," all of which was long overdue. Its section 15(2), however, sanctioned affirmative action programs. Soon after, groups organized by gender, colour, sexual orientation, and ethnicity began to exert themselves and to demand their due rights and privileges, and political correctness began to develop. With stunning rapidity, the Charter notwithstanding, the freedom to speak, act, and write gradually became constrained in almost every area of Canadian life. There were antismoking bans, conferences of "writers of colour" from which whites were barred, the denunciation of anyone who questioned the "repressed memory syndrome," calls for a prohibition on research in whole areas of science relating to human reproduction, and a host of additional examples that go on indefinitely.

Somehow, perhaps because they have been emboldened by the Charter, some groups, commissions, jurists, and individuals have created a categorization of rights. If you do this, you are trampling on my rights. My rights, in other words, are superior to your rights; my memories of past ills take precedence over yours; and my right to privacy outweighs your right to know. All of these areas are contentious and all can be debated endlessly. What is certain, however, is that the state has encouraged groups and individuals to intrude into areas that were hitherto sacrosanct. In the guise of tolerance, intolerance has been accepted and become government policy. In the guise of justice, injustice has stepped in. In the guise of open speech, doublespeak has become the norm. Humanity may have made it past 1984, but the Orwellian world is with us still.

Universities are both a part of and a reflection of the society in which they operate. But there is one important difference that makes universities stand out. Universities boast of their academic freedom, of their professors' right to contemplate any subject and to speak out on every issue, without fear of censorship or of being fired. Free inquiry is the reason for existence of academe, and rightly so. Many of the great discoveries in science and the important ideas in the humanities and social sciences have emerged in the face of public disbelief or opprobrium. If conformity is rammed down the throats of teachers and thinkers, the results will be serious for the development of our society.

The universities' main clientele is young and energetic, and the enthusiasms of youth are legion and legend, so the waves of opinion that affect society often wash with tsunami-like force over the universities. Students believe they are trend-setters. They may be in music and fashion, but not necessarily in ideas, and especially not in this conservative era. Anything that challenges the received version is viewed with suspicion by huge numbers of youth. And because professors are notoriously woolly minded and ideologically driven, there are always scholars ready and willing to pronounce their benedictions on the actions of their students.

———————

Consider the case of J. Philippe Rushton of the University of Western Ontario in London, Ontario. A research psychologist, Rushton had competed for and won some of the best research grants open to scholars in North America. He was considered one of the stars in a strong department — until he did research on racial differences.

In the late 1980s Rushton began to study the differences among whites, Orientals, and blacks, his research leading him to compare such traits as brain size, performance on standardized tests, personality and temperament, social behaviour, maturation, sexual habits, and fertility. His conclusions, roughly speaking, were that blacks on average were more fertile, faster maturing, more sexually active, and less accomplished in standard tests than Orientals, who tended towards the opposite in each of these areas. Whites, he found, fell between the other two groups. All these findings were presented, properly enough, as a hypothesis.

This area of research is well beyond the competence of three Canadian historians to evaluate, and we are obviously unable to tell if Rushton's hypothesis is sound or utter poppycock. The usually sensible Michael Keefer, the University of Guelph English professor whose 1992 book *Lunar Perspectives: Field Notes from the Culture Wars*, pours soft soap on troubled academic waters, however, has no hesitation in pronouncing Rushton's work "racialist pseudoscience." What is clear is that the psychologist's choice of subject was risky, and his conclusions doubly so.

What Rushton reported deeply angered students, faculty, the public, and politicians. The firestorm began when he presented a paper to the American Association for the Advancement of Science in January 1989 in which he laid out the areas of difference he had found among the races. Black groups in London began to protest as soon as they learned of this paper, and on 2 February the Premier of Ontario, David Peterson, whose home town was London, denounced Rushton's work as "highly questionable, destructive, and offensive to the way Ontario thinks." Two weeks later the *Toronto Star* suggested that Rushton was an inept fraud whose research was financed by the "Nazi" Pioneer Fund, an American granting agency, and published by a racist journal, *The Mankind Quarterly*.

Rushton's dean, an anthropologist who is now the president of the University of Manitoba, declared that the psychologist had lost all scientific credibility; his department chair, in the same year that Rushton won a prized Guggenheim fellowship, denied him the progress-through-the-ranks pay increase that an annual review should have brought him; and the Ontario Provincial Police began to question his colleagues and students as part of a six-month investigation to see if he had broken Canadian anti-hate laws. The attorney general of Ontario, however, concluded that Rushton's research, while incompetent, was not criminal. The newly created Academic Coalition for Equity at the university collected a thousand signatures of faculty and students and called for the establishment of a committee to prevent "scientific racism within the curriculum of the university." A large number of academics around the country, including some with competence in the area in question, stepped forward to denounce Rushton's findings.

Before long, Rushton's tenured position was in doubt and the university had two separate investigations under way on the ethics of his experiments with students. University administrators threatened to monitor his classes to ensure they were not racist, and when demonstrators began to picket, his department demanded that he teach his large lecture course via videotape. In 1991, efforts to drive Rushton out having failed, a complaint by nineteen present and former students was made to the Ontario Human Rights Commission that the psychologist had "poisoned the academic learning environment" with his teaching and research. This complaint stayed under investigation until 1995, when it was finally dropped. The only useful event in this horrific process was that alarmed colleagues in Rushton's Department of Psychology set up the Society for Academic Freedom and Scholarship as an organization to crusade for free speech and untrammelled research.

None of Rushton's critics within the university or the media, or among politicians or the public, emerged from this affair with any glory. To his credit, however, the president of the University of Western Ontario argued that while Rushton's views did not represent those of the university, he could not accept the demands for Rushton's immediate dismissal. At least one vice-president sturdily defended Rushton's academic freedom to do research in areas and in ways that he chose. "The university is not based on the premise," Tom Collins told a meeting of the university's senate, "that there is an academic or political press or public [that] decide that...this scientist has offended society. The judgments will be made, but not this way." The critics, however, were angered all the more. To use academic freedom to defend Rushton was to pervert it, they claimed. The theories he espoused were not true, and academic freedom was valid only if it protects the truth.

But what if Rushton's hypotheses were true? Even that was no defence. David Suzuki, the well-known CBC science expert and geneticist, debated Rushton on television and argued that "in a society in which racism is rampant it is not sufficient for a scientist to say 'I am merely giving you truth.'" In other words, if he was telling racist lies, he was guilty; if he was telling the truth, that was no defence, given the uses to which such unpleasant truths could be put.

This argument is utter nonsense. The duty of scientists like Philippe Rushton and David Suzuki is to develop a research-based hypothesis and to propound the results in open scholarly forums. If others disagree with the hypothesis advanced, they are free to challenge it and, out of the debate, a new synthesis can emerge which in turn will eventually come under attack. Traditionally, that is the way scholarship has advanced, and it is only when Stalinists or Hitlerites have declared that their version of truth is absolute that science has led to disaster. In Ontario in 1989, the premier of Ontario pronounced that a scientific hypothesis was destructive and offensive. Deans and faculty members, students and members of the public argued that all research that suggested there were differences among races was by definition wrong, especially if it found that one race was different from a second.

Rushton's critics were arguing that a whole area of research should be forbidden. Race, however important it might be in human life, could not be studied — unless one set out to show that all races were equal. But if race is a forbidden subject, then it is surely only a matter of time before some government or university or newspaper or public group declares that Marxism, having fallen from power almost everywhere in the world, is no longer to be studied. Why the professors and students, most standing on the left, who attacked Rushton did not see where their position led was unclear. The blind apparently can never see where they are headed and, lemming-like, the crowd plunged over the precipice, all but legitimizing the attack that some day was sure to be directed against them. In all likelihood, the only people who will defend the Marxist left when its proscription is demanded will be the same believers in free speech who defended Philippe Rushton.

It was not only in Ontario that political correctness raged. Consider the case of Matin Yaqzan, a tenured assistant professor of mathematics at Fredericton's University of New Brunswick for twenty-seven years. Yaqzan's case is interesting because it contrasts so clearly with Rushton's. Unlike Rushton, Yaqzan was no well-published scholar, as his life-long rank of assistant professor demonstrated, but he was a loud-mouthed commentator on a range of political and university issues, many of his positions being notably foolish. Even so, he had never shouted the equivalent of "fire" in a crowded theatre, the classic definition of actionable speech. Thus, no one paid much attention to Yaqzan until November 1993, when he wrote an article in the campus student newspaper on date rape.

The math professor said that if a woman visited a man's room after hours she might be seen as accepting sexual intercourse. After all, if a woman was in his room, a young man for whom sexual intercourse was a necessity might well believe that she was "tacitly consenting." The date rape of such a woman was more of an "inconvenience" than a "moral outrage," Yaqzan went on. Moreover, sexually promiscuous women "would not suffer as a result of an unwanted sexual encounter to the same degree as a girl for whom it might be the first sexual experience." When raped, therefore, "a promiscuous girl...would be more reasonable...to demand some monetary compensation for inconvenience or discomfort rather than express moral outrage."

The student, public, and university response was one of shock. Every women's organization on campus and in the province protested, the student council urged that Yaqzan be disciplined, and the university's student safety officer characterized his article as an "incitement to violence against women," which it was not. Those remarks, however, fed the panic, the administration became frightened, and UNB's president wrote to every newspaper in New Brunswick to denounce Yaqzan. Despite the guarded support Yaqzan received from the UNB faculty association, the professor was suspended. The protection for academic freedom in the collective agreement between the university and its faculty was not violated, UNB said, as the suspension merely provided "a cooling off period so that public safety and an orderly academic environment" could be maintained. Yaqzan was barred from his office and the campus by court injunction, and threatened with an administrative review of everything he might have ever said in his classes. In the furore, the fact that there had been no complaints about his teaching and no suggestion it was anything but satisfactory was immaterial. Like Rushton, whom he resembled in no other way, Yaqzan was punished as if he had committed heinous crimes.

Why? Nothing he said was illegal in any way, however foolish it may have been. One can argue that Yaqzan, as a professor, was in a position of trust and that male students might conceivably take his article as licence to act brutally to women. One can also argue, more forcefully, that women students must have the right to go wherever they choose, including dormitory rooms, whenever they choose, including late at night, without fear of having their actions misconstrued as an invitation to sexual intercourse. Nonetheless, the university's action was a direct threat to the freedom of speech of everyone on campus. "If suddenly any one of us makes a comment that the president or vice-president doesn't like," one political scientist said, "then are we going to be subject to dismissal or suspension?" UNB's actions had debased the academic freedom of all its faculty.

Although his suspension was lifted after two weeks, Yaqzan chose to accept an early retirement buy-out rather than be subjected to the threatened hearings. The ultimate comment on the case came not from the Canadian Association of University Teachers, which was all but silent, but from Alan Borovoy of the Canadian Civil Liberties Association. Free speech demands that sometimes you must go "to bat for the freedom of speech of somebody you don't like, somebody who's unpopular. It may mean a Yaqzan." Borovoy added that opinions expressed in a campus newspaper must receive debate, not employment sanctions. Borovoy was precisely right. Nothing Yaqzan wrote merited the response it received. Undoubtedly, what he had written was offensive, deeply so, but offensive speech, writings, and actions do not deserve the pillory, and certainly not in a university. All across Canada, the distinction between offensive and actionable speech and writing seemed to have blurred.

Then in 1993 Ontario's NDP government put all the province's universities on alert: employment equity had become the policy of choice, and large employers were directed to ensure that their workforces reflected the racial composition of the locality in which they operated. The universities began to ask faculty and staff to indicate their racial origin and gender, and whether they were disabled. Most faculty tamely filled in the forms, but that was not enough for the universities. With the quiet issuance of its "zero-tolerance" guidelines against harassment and discrimination in the province's universities, the Ministry of Education and Training undertook what University of Western Ontario law professor Robert Martin called "the most thorough and far-reaching attempt to place express limits on research and academic discourse in Canada." Faculty and students alike had their rights to talk and argue about issues of consequence curtailed.

Freedom of speech and academic freedom were less important in the eyes of the NDP government than the need to protect students and faculty from discrimination because of race, creed, sex, sexual orientation, disability, age, dialect, accent, the receipt of public assistance, record of provincial offences or pardoned federal offences, and harassment, including sexual harassment. Harassment was defined as "something that is known or might reasonably be known to be offensive, hostile, and inappropriate, including gestures, remarks, jokes, taunting, innuendo, display of offensive materials." Another offence was creation of a "negative environment," and the guidelines made clear that "a complainant does not have to be a direct target to be adversely affected by a negative environment."

Consider how this extraordinary policy might affect a classroom discussion. If, for example, a professor criticized Quebec independence in a political science class at the bilingual University of Ottawa, a sovereignist student might feel that a negative, indeed hostile, environment had been created. A study of literature — *The Scarlet Letter*, for example, or *The Merchant of Venice* — could lead to complaints by women or Jewish students. A class in feminism might make a male student feel that he had been excluded. Worse still, the guidelines extended off campus to include all places students and/or faculty might meet, and they explicitly covered campus newspapers and radio stations.

When the guidelines finally became public (thanks to Professors Martin at Western and John Fekete of Trent University, and columnist Robert Fulford in the *Globe and Mail*), the minister of education backed off slightly. What was depressing, however, with a very few honourable exceptions, was the way university administrations and faculty associations accepted this most blatant attack on academic freedom and the role of the university. There were a few belated critical comments from the Canadian Association of University Teachers, though one opined that the minister's "heart was in the right place," and there was a weak call for delay in implementation. However, most of CAUT's component faculty associations in Ontario said little or expressed approval. York University Faculty Association's Ad Hoc Committee on Sexual Harassment, for example, told the university that "we support the spirit of the document." To oppose offensive speech, the unchecked battle of ideas, was obviously too risky in 1990s Ontario. The guidelines were withdrawn, in a manner of speaking, in February 1994, but they have not yet been definitively buried.

———————

In fact, the Ontario guidelines were already entrenched inside Canadian universities. What used to be considered inappropriate behaviour was now sexual harassment, and there were sexual harassment officers stationed on every campus to ensure that miscreants were investigated and prosecuted. In addition, almost all campuses had some or all of the following offices and officers: associate vice-presidents (equity), race relations and anti-racism initiatives officers, employment equity officers, First Nations houses, personal safety awareness officers, and status of women officers, the list comprising a virtual catalogue of every hot button issue of the 1990s. Each of these officers and offices cost money — at the University of Toronto the estimate at the university level for salaries, staff, and office space was $1.5 million a year, with additional sums expended by the faculties and colleges — or roughly the equivalent of forty junior faculty at $40,000 a year. Many came to believe that the officers sought out complainants to justify their existence.

What was worse, in many cases elemental fairness was lacking in the way complaints were investigated. One trumped-up case of sexual harassment at King's College of the University of Western Ontario put a psychology professor through the wringer for a year, denied him the right to confront his accusers, and made him wait months before he learned he had been cleared. The faculty association essentially supported the administration's position, and the Ontario Confederation of University Faculty Associations and the Canadian Association of University Teachers refused to lend the then dues-paying professor any assistance. In the eyes of faculty and students, but happily not many of the students in the professor's class, the accusation of harassment was tantamount to guilt. In all its odiousness, zero tolerance obviously existed before the Ontario guidelines. In the end, King's College paid the professor's legal fees and gave him a year's paid leave, an expensive way for the Ontario taxpayers to atone for the unendurable and the inexcusable. No action of any kind was taken against those students making the false allegations of misbehaviour.

Such Star Chamber procedures unfortunately are closer to the norm than we might wish, as a female professor of Spanish at the University of Western Ontario discovered when an innocent remark she made in class offended an Iranian student. The professor was dragged through expensive hearings, only to be completely vindicated and awarded her costs and a year off to recover. No action was taken against the student. And in one case at the University of Manitoba, when a professor charged with sexual harassment resigned rather than be put through a hearing, a university official said smugly: "He did not respond. He did not deny. If you don't deny, it's the same thing as accepting [guilt]." Zero tolerance in Manitoba, too.

The climate in the universities today has made all these cases into daily fare in the campus press. The sense has been created that there is a male culture of bullies, boors, and bigots that so dominates higher education that it must be confronted, assaulted, attacked, and ultimately destroyed. Hence the support for zero tolerance in Ontario. In an article in 1992 in *Canadian Women's Studies*, one author summed it all up: "Women in Canadian universities inhabit a hostile and sexist environment. Manifestations of sexism may be subtle: the suspicious absence of women from curriculum; the invisibility of women in positions of power within the institutional hierarchy; and the low percentage of female faculty. Other manifestations...may be more blatant: sexual assaults on campus; sexual harassment by male professors and male students; and misogynist initiation rituals." A hostile and sexist environment indeed. But where? That men are often sexist is undeniable. But could the situation genuinely be as bad as painted?

If one believes the Status of Women Committee of the Canadian Association of University Teachers, there can be no doubt that we are in crisis. In annual supplements to CAUT's bulletin, publications presumably published with the approval of CAUT, the Status of Women Committee has challenged the operations, not to say the very existence, of universities as they are known in Canada. The universities are terrifying places to the writers in these supplements, physically threatening, routinely demeaning to women, and managed by patriarchal administrators whose main goal is to keep women out of faculty positions and to suppress or minimize feminist studies in the academy. Against these forces, women faculty struggle for the "inclusive university," a place where truth (but only one kind of truth) will prevail and where all, women and men, white and black, straight and gay, will feel comfortable in the absence of offensive teachers, students, and other varieties of thought.

A perfect example of this approach is found in the article in the 1994 *Supplement* by Carleton University Canadian Studies professor Jill Vickers, "Are Efforts to Renovate the Concept of Academic Freedom Useful?" Vickers had attended university as an undergraduate in the 1950s, and she began by recalling the sexist teaching styles of the males who had taught her, professors who had simply destroyed the confidence of other women students. Then as a junior instructor, she discovered that an anthropology professor's exam asked "students to document the case for the arguments that blacks had no soul." The possibility that this might have been a teaching technique is not considered; it was blatant racism. Her teaching would be different, she vowed, and in her Canadian Studies school at Carleton she undertook a "textbook audit":

> A group of students and faculty examined all the textbooks we were using in our classes, looking for sexist, racist, etc., biases. An aboriginal student was very concerned that one of our texts taught that aboriginal peoples came to North America over the Bering Strait from Asia. I argued that it seemed to be a "proven scientific fact." He responded that aboriginal peoples believed that they had originated on this continent — that is that they were indigenous. I asked if the two positions could be taught as parallel "belief systems"? He responded that some scientists questioned the Bering thesis and that it was often used to "prove" that aboriginal peoples were also "immigrants" to the Americas and consequently that their claims to their lands were no different than the claims of later immigrants... We are still struggling with this issue together, as a *community*, with as much civility as we can muster ...As university faculty, we must come to realize that we have responsibilities which are at least as important as our rights and that we are responsible for responding sincerely and creatively to the challenges of diversity with mutual respect.

This explanation was in keeping with the main position paper in the *Supplement* which suggested that "the protection of academic freedom in the practice of exclusion has...denied students access to their histories, their experiences, and to knowledge — the knowledge of non-Western, non-white, and non-male scholarship."

Vickers' approach is frankly terrifying. First, that Vickers and her colleagues and students would survey all texts to eliminate anything and everything that did not meet her bias-free criteria is simply wrong. A university is a place for the clash of ideas, and if the texts have biases (even a feminist text might have some!), then any good teacher could use them to make a point of value to students. Second, as the example of the aboriginal student's concerns make clear, one person's scientific fact may well be another's perception of bias. That North American aboriginal peoples did cross over the Bering Strait is fact, exactly as Vickers noted; that she would agree to the construction of "parallel belief systems" is a shocking abdication of her responsibility as a teacher. The aboriginal student, in Vickers' conception of the university, should not be made to grapple with inconvenient fact; instead, the student should be encouraged to believe that his view was as valid as her own. To avoid offence, the teacher was prepared to abandon truth. And this is a university? Third, to remove all bias, all points of view, from texts is to create mush, pap fit only for spoonfeeding. But there is no doubt that the Vickers of the world are winning. Every province has its rules and regulations on what cannot — and must be — said in its high school textbooks; university books so far have been exempt, but the "bias"-seekers are making headway. That is why at least one author of this book will never write another textbook.

The concluding paper in the *Supplement*, by law professor Jennifer Bankier of Dalhousie University, praised Vickers' sensitivity and referred to her anecdotes drawn from her own experience. Vickers had provided "some concrete examples of the kind of speech that has a destructive impact on the academic freedom of students through gratuitous attacks on their values, safety, knowledge, and competence in the classroom or on examination...On the basis of these examples, she argues for greater responsibility, reciprocity, and sensitivity to power relationships on the part of faculty." All of us have favourite anecdotes; some of us dine out regularly on them. But no scholar bases history and policy prescriptions on anecdotal evidence, refined in the telling and distorted by the passage of years, especially when it leads directly to the views that Vickers propounds with her book-banning and anti-scientific practices.

We might wish that Vickers was a unique case, but she is not. The CAUT *Bulletin* and the Status of Women Committee Supplements are full of similar anti-scholarly cant. We are told that the past fruits of intellectual endeavour are "socially-constructed ideas" that "strut about to parade as absolute concepts in academic robes....they were framed by a patriarchal power structure that is also white, able-bodied, hetero-sexual and middle class," all of which are swear words. We are told that women's scholarship "is evaluated upon standards of excellence based upon male models," as if excellence and academic quality were some-how different for women than for men.[2] We are urged to support the "woman-friendly" university — a university that would emphasize, among other things, "a balance in course content with regard to male and female scholarship, perspectives and concerns" and require all stu-dents to take at least one women's studies course as a requirement for graduation. We are told that gender balance in the faculty should be achieved within five years and that departments that fail to meet this criterion should be disciplined. And we are told that the speech and behaviour of (male) faculty should be reformed in mandatory work-shops on sexual harassment, sexual violence, and the negative effects of subtle discrimination. Moreover, gender-neutral language (fishers not

---

2. Sometimes they seem to be, not least in law, one area where feminist scholarship has made an impact. Two examples: in 1992 Professor Hester Lessard referred to the "systemic racism implicit in legal reasoning based on precedent" as fact — she apparently saw no need to provide any proof whatsoever; systemic racism, of course, needed no definition. And Professor Diana Majury of Carleton University's Department of Law explained why she had *refused to read* a judicial decision about which she was writing: "I have not read the Court of Appeal deci-sion. Having read about it and heard about it, I chose not to put myself through the pain of reading it." Both comments were in scholarly publications that were either refereed or at least edited according to alleged scholarly standards.

fishermen, labour not manpower, and compulsory use of she/he?) should be required in all communications. All this is intended to make the university more comfortable for women, homosexuals, the differently abled, and non-whites.

The result has been widespread self-censorship. One Simon Fraser University professor wrote:

> I use Darwin's theory of evolution in my teaching and research. My courses entail discussing the evolutionary significance of altruism, mating, crime, coercive sexuality and war. For many years I taught this material without fear about whether my audiences felt "comfortable." Recently, I was taken to task by a woman for using the phrase "if your father is a doctor." She said it demeaned her because it implied that women could not become doctors. Lately, I have eliminated some material from my courses. I tape all my lectures so there can be no question of what I say in class. I try to restrain my sense of humour. I say things about white males that might get me into trouble if I said them about members of marginalized groups...I explain that though students must understand the ideas I present, they need not believe them. I tell them some of my ideas may be wrong. So far my tactics for avoiding trouble have been adequate.

This same professor, one who has fought to preserve free inquiry, added that the greatest threat to academic freedom "comes from those who would use university harassment policies to censor ideas and the language in which they are expressed." He has put his finger on precisely the critical point if universities are to survive as centres of free inquiry. Teaching about some subjects makes some people uncomfortable, so such teaching should be censored. "It follows," he notes, "that harassment policies should take precedence over academic freedom. I claim that the opposite is true." So do we. Academic freedom must take precedence over harassment policies.

CAUT no longer appears to agree with this approach. In its Ad Hoc Committee Report on Employment Equity of April 1994, CAUT stated that "instructors should design their courses carefully so as not to be racist, homophobic or misogynist...Departments, faculties and senates should review course descriptions and programmes on a regular basis to ensure that no group is inappropriately marginalized." Of course, CAUT maintains, this does not interfere with academic freedom. What the Committee Report fails to understand, however, is that feelings of marginalization are almost wholly subjective. Smith may feel marginalized by your comment, but Jones may not, for example. Moreover, as Harvey Shulman, vice-president of the Concordia University faculty association wrote, it is completely unacceptable for CAUT to depict academics as silencers of diversity and perpetrators of marginalization, just as it is improper for CAUT to urge mandatory reviews to evaluate curriculum. Once the door is opened to such reviews, what ideas will someday be declared improper? Under the impulse of equity and inoffensiveness to all, CAUT has lost its way — and its credibility. The whole atmosphere in Canadian universities had been distorted.[3]

But the advocates of zero tolerance were by no means finished. In their view, universities suffered from a "chilly climate" for women, non-white faculty, students, and other marginalized groups. How could one recognize a chilly climate? An article in the 1996 Status of

---

3. A perfect example of distortion is the *Report of the Ryerson Faculty Association Equity Issues Committee on Employment Systems at Ryerson Polytechnic University* (1996). Relentlessly pursuing equity and relevance, the committee urged the Toronto university to adopt a policy of "equity and representativeness" that in practice appeared to mean that only blacks could teach black history, or Asians, Asian history. The curriculum, the report argued, had to be relevant to the community and, since the community was diverse, the faculty must be diverse as well. That an Asian could teach electrical engineering to whites or a black teach Canadian history to Asian students seemed a foreign concept to a faculty association that wore rose-coloured multicultural blinkers.

Women Committee *Supplement* by Susan Prentice of the University of Winnipeg's Canadian Studies department provided a handy guide. A chilly climate is a systemic condition — wherever there is no hard evidence, one can be certain that the word "systemic" will be wheeled into battle — with the following characteristics:

- representation: the exclusion of women and people of colour and the over-representation of white males;
- marginalization: the concentration of women and people of colour in positions of powerlessness and the over-privileged positions of white men;
- meritocracy: the belief that in a meritocratic university, characteristics such as sex and race are immaterial; and
- academic freedom: defined as an individual rather than a collective right; overt sexism, for example, can be frowned on, but anti-feminism will be tolerated as freedom of expression.

If this is the definition of chilly climate, the authors of this book will clearly be lumped in with the defenders of the freeze. While we do not support the exclusion of anyone from positions of administrative power in the university on grounds of gender or race, we certainly oppose the rejection of merit and academic freedom employed by Prentice. Indeed, such concepts threaten the very existence of universities as centres of knowledge, debate, study, and the striving after excellence. Some Canadian academics are waging a war, and nowhere has this battle been fought with more heat — and less light — than in British Columbia.

———————

The story begins at the University of Victoria. The Department of Political Science was a small one until the early 1990s, just eight men. But by 1992 it had begun to adapt to the new realities on Canadian campuses and had hired three women faculty. Then, trying to be "fair," it asked one of the new faculty members, Somer Brodribb, to talk and work with women students. Brodribb's subsequent report from "The Committee to Make the Department More Supportive to Women" (it was better known as the Chilly Climate Committee, a committee apparently made up of Brodribb and five female students) was completed in March 1993. In describing the "chilly climate" in the department, it alleged that women faculty and students were regularly subjected to sexist and racist comments, that some faculty had criticized feminist ideas (twelve of twenty complaints in the report dealt with this issue), and that there had been cases of male faculty sexually harassing students. No names were attached to the allegations, and there was no evidence of a systematic survey of opinion in the report, but the male faculty, hitherto sharply divided ideologically, came together as one with a demand for "credible evidence to support these assertions" of sexual harassment or the retraction of the offending paragraph. If this was not done, the professors threatened "further steps" to protect their standing in the community. The result was the virtual paralysis, not to say destruction, of a department when the charges of sexism ran head on into determined calls for due process.

Victoria's president soon struck a two-person investigating committee, consisting of former judge Tom Berger and Ruth Bilson, a Saskatchewan law professor, that issued a seventy-page report in January 1994. The committee said it could not discern how Brodribb's committee had proceeded and it insisted that future allegations of harassment be funnelled through the university's existing procedures. "No one," the investigators wrote, "wishes to discount the collective experience of women. One should, however, be able to have some confidence that what is being described is the experience of the collective, not merely of a few." Moreover, "feminists, conscious of the power of words, should deploy [words like sexism and racism] with precision, and with an acute awareness of their implications." The male professors did not escape scot free, but the report's criticism of them was mild: their threat of "further steps" had ended any possibility of compromise.

From our point of view, the Berger-Bilson report was an important check to unsubstantiated claims of harassment, sexism, and racism and a blow to the Chilly Climate talk. Moreover, we believe that the male professors' threat of further action was not only justified but necessary. No one should be obliged to put up with a smear campaign that threatens reputations and livelihoods, and anyone who sets out to libel and slander individuals has to be ready to prove the case. The result was a victory of sorts for good sense, but, regrettably, the University of Victoria department lay in ruins, with one of the women faculty on stress leave, a second boycotting committee meetings in protest, and Brodribb seeking a transfer to the Women's Studies department; she was later briefly suspended by the university for failing to comply with its sick-leave policy. The male faculty survived the attack, though academic reputations that had taken years to build were all but ruined and a cloud continued to hang over the department. And faculty, student, and administration time, weeks and months of time, continued to be swallowed up by the on-going repercussions, legal and otherwise, of the Chilly Climate Committee's work.

Bloody as the University of Victoria battle was, however, it was merely a warm-up for the battle on the BC mainland. The University of British Columbia, one of the country's premier universities, suffered from many of the same sorts of sexual and racial harassment issues that troubled campuses in the 1990s. Women students in residence were the targets of obscene notes in 1990, an incident that produced demonstrations and the eventual suspension of seventeen students for periods ranging from four to sixteen months; in 1993 threatening anti-feminist letters were sent to the university's counselling psychology department; and in 1992 there was a sharp debate over the "Draft Policy on Human Rights" that circulated among faculty for comment. Peter Suedfeld, a distinguished psychologist and then the dean of graduate studies, for one, objected to the absence of any provision in the draft to protect the rights of faculty "to teach facts (much less opinions) that might be unwelcome to some 'individual or group.' Presumably, faculty members could be subjected to investigation or hearings if a student in their class objects to being taught that some cultures have in the past practised cannibalism, slavery, or human sacrifice; or that women on the average score lower than men on measures of some abilities (and vice versa)…There is to be no freedom at UBC for reporting 'unwelcome' data, discussing heretical theories, or making remarks designed to provoke discussion or controversy (and thought)." His and other complaints helped push the draft policy into a form more acceptable to those who worried about academic freedom and the proper role of universities.

Unfortunately, this concern for academic freedom was quickly forgotten. In June 1995 a 175-page report, prepared at a cost of almost $247,000 by lawyer and self-described "human rights complaints investigator; harassment analyst; [and] troubleshooter" Joan McEwen pilloried the UBC Department of Political Science. The story began in 1992 when a dozen mostly female graduate students wrote an anonymous nine-page memo alleging "pervasive racism and sexism" as well as hostility to feminist theory in the department. Despite the fact that anonymous allegations ought not to have been worth the paper they were printed on, and despite efforts by the department chair to reconcile matters and to counter the allegations of racism, the students remained fixed in their view. In another memo, they proclaimed that "the first symptom of racism is to deny that it exists." Using this standard, all "not guilty" pleas are proof positive of culpability. By the summer of 1994, the issue had become serious enough that the university appointed McEwen to investigate. Ten months later, after soliciting information through, among other ways, posters titled "Pervasive Racism and Sexism in the Political Science Department," McEwen issued her report. She had written in an article in 1995 that "there is a trend in British Columbia towards a less formal way of resolving workplace disputes" and this, she said, is a trend to be encouraged. "The more parties… can fashion 'grass roots,' 'win-win' models of dispute resolution…the greater the potential for tailor-made solutions which actually 'work' for all concerned over the long term." Win-win was not the way anyone could describe McEwen's report.

Her "warlock" hunt predictably found evidence to support the allegations of racism and sexism. In her report, however, no names were attached either to those making the allegations or the supposed perpetrators, and none of the allegations cited was pronounced specifically true or false. But of the general condition there was no doubt. Guilty as charged, McEwen wrote. There was both direct and systemic discrimination, sexism, and racism, she said, though none of these terms were defined. One male professor had asked students for dates and made unwanted sexual advances. A professor had invited a student to "discuss her paper" over dinner, while another had necked conspicuously with a student around the department. A professor in a class had compared a temperamental photocopy machine to a woman. A professor had told a graduate student that being a woman would help her get a job, but that her being older would not. A limited-term professor had joked to a black graduate student that her tough grading would likely lead students to see her as "one big, bad, black bitch."

The list of complaints was seemingly endless, and the comments, collected in interviews, ranged from the trivial to the banal to the grave. But in the spirit of the age, all were treated as equally serious. While there was no reason to believe that any individual professor was actually prejudiced or had intended to discriminate, McEwen wrote, nonetheless the culture of the department "may well have an adverse impact on those students who do not share its prevailing characteristics" — that is, "the older, white, male, heterosexual, middle class, of Anglo/European cultural heritage." Evidence from students who did not share the view that the department was riddled with bias and sexism was shunted aside and given no weight at all.

Receiving the report, UBC's president David Strangway said there would be no disciplinary action against any of the twenty-five professors in the department, and no students would be compensated. By disciplinary, Strangway and his associates seem to have meant they would do nothing to bring on arbitrations or formal investigations, though it was open season on reputations. Still, McEwen's recommendation that no more graduate students be admitted in political science until the climate in the department improved was accepted. No such sanction had ever been imposed on a department in any university in Canada, and it is hard to avoid the conclusion that, completely rattled, Strangway had panicked. In effect, the whole political science department had been found guilty of racism and sexism by UBC's president; so, too, by implication, given the way McEwen's report presumed that all white males were almost by definition prejudiced, were the majority of UBC's faculty. As Sandra Martin wrote on 28 September 1996 in the *Globe and Mail*, Strangway had silenced one of his departments "and he does it in the guise of freedom of expression."

Within days, the reaction had taken form. The head of the UBC faculty association, a law professor, denounced the McEwen report's methodology, noting that there was no indication if statements were based on eyewitness testimony or rumours. "The report," he said, "fails to identify what evidence supports which complaint and to indicate how strong the evidence was for various complaints." In fact, this was precisely true — the McEwen report was a compendium of allegations, all of which appeared to receive equal weight. McEwen had failed to exercise even the most basic effort to prove the truth or falsity of the allegations. To her, as to the students who had lodged the complaints, it mattered not whether the allegations were true. If the students believed them, that was sufficient. This stress on perception over reality discredited her report completely.

So too did the comments in the press in Canada and around the world, most notably in the *Globe and Mail,* which quickly made a crusade of the UBC case. The report was pronounced "a bone-chilling document" that had reduced UBC to "the most cringing conformity." Columnist Margaret Wente pronounced McEwen's study "a tragedy for female students. How well will they be mentored now, when professors are afraid to talk to them outside class, afraid to criticize their work, afraid to give them realistic career advice?" The dean of arts, Patricia Marchak, who had been the first to demand an investigation as well as a member of the administration group that had recommended hiring McEwen and set her terms of reference, soon weighed in, calling the report "deeply flawed." The BC Civil Liberties Association used similar words in its comment, which also added that Strangway's action in stopping graduate admissions in political science had "created a 'chill' on academic freedom which will be felt for many years...across North America."

But other UBC professors, some of whom recognized the flaws in the report, declared that any errors did not outweigh its content. "It can't be ignored [just] because it is flawed," said one senior woman historian. Three more well-established women academics in an extraordinary letter in the Vancouver *Sun*, while professing allegiance to the core values of the university, nonetheless argued that such values as knowledge and tolerance had been "historically employed to exclude and marginalize disadvantaged groups including women, people of colour, native people and gays and lesbians." Again and again, they said,

> we hear the voices of white male professors claiming persecution by 'intemperate' women and people of colour. In these tirades, white males remain the universal unmarked standard of discourse and behaviour. Every one else, it seems, is engaged in narrow, self-interest 'identity' politics. These professors ignore their own history of privilege and the benefits they have received from exclusionary practices and, instead, expropriate the language of victimization.
>
> Demands for more inclusive universities, which practise the pluralism they preach, threaten the faculty's right to unilaterally set curricula and research agendas without regard to consequences in the classroom or the perpetuation of partial understandings.

If any other group — black women, Asian males, aboriginals — had been assailed in such terms, calls for prosecution under Canada's anti-hate laws would likely have been heard; white males, however, were fair game. But what was most astonishing in this letter was the call to let someone, anyone, other than (white male) faculty set curricula and research agendas. Did this trio propose to permit the students to determine what is studied? Community groups?[4] Themselves?

One of the letter writers, historian Veronica Strong-Boag, also denounced contemporary universities for having "helped to rationalize imperialism, capitalism, racism and sexism in the service of Europe's and North America's expansionary states." Moreover, she added, the universities commonly persecuted those who "championed the equality of the sexes, the classes, and the races" — by giving them secure tenured jobs and high salaries, presumably. The dean of graduate studies, a white male who obviously wallowed joyously in self-abnegation, said in equally disgraceful terms that universities "have been dominated by senior white male faculty members. It is not surprising, but unacceptable, for this group to seek to perpetuate its domination of our University," words that should have been enough to justify his immediate firing. Faculty privilege could not be allowed to impede students' access to a hospitable learning environment, he said. God forbid that any idea should cause offence to anyone — except, of course, white males.

Individuals and organizations outside UBC soon got into the act. Judy Rebick, former head of the National Action Committee on the Status of Women and present-day TV performer, argued that the outcry against the "whipping girl" of the McEwen report "served as a cover for anyone in the department who might actually be guilty of sexual harassment." Anyone but Rebick might have thought that the purpose of McEwen's report was to discover such individuals and not to smear the entire male complement of political science. To its credit, CAUT overcame the feminist lobby within its ranks and politely denounced the denial of due process to the political science faculty. The UBC administration, CAUT said, "decided to suspend the intake of

---

4. UBC's Sikh Studies professor was soon in difficulty with his community leaders, who objected to the line his research followed. They had put up some of the money for his chair (the rest coming from multiculturalism funds from Ottawa) and believed they had the right to control his output. Other "ethnic studies" chairs in many universities faced similar difficulties.

students into the graduate program in Political Science without verify-
ing Ms. McEwen's allegations."

There was more to be revealed of the UBC affair. One of the first
students to charge sexual and racial harassment had taken her claims to
the BC Council of Human Rights but, it turned out, had said she would
be willing to drop her complaint if certain terms were met, including
the following: the guaranteed completion of her MA and acceptance
into the PhD program; $40,000 for tuition and expenses (subsequently
raised to $50,000); that only named individuals be on her dissertation
committee; that two course grades be removed and replaced with
"pass"; and that she be given six "acceptable" letters of recommendation
on the completion of her MA. We can imagine the anxious debates that
must have taken place in the president's office on receipt of this missive,
but this was too much even for Strangway. The demands were rejected.

The complainants were not yet through. In September 1995 their
demands, as presented by one female graduate student (who left the
graduate program in August), escalated to include a formal apology to
be signed by each professor acknowledging his sexism and racism and
his willingness to take a twelve-step recovery program of twelve weekly
mandatory workshops. (These demands were an amazing combination
of Alcoholics Anonymous and the treatment meted out to reactionaries
during Chairman Mao's 1960s cultural revolution!) Any professor who
refused these demands should be offered early retirement. There
should be a new department head hired from outside the province, and
incompetent professors should be stopped from teaching. "Unlimited
numbers" of letters of reference were to be made available to graduate
students, and students should have a majority on all department committees. The ranking of graduate students should also cease (which
would mean an end to competitive MA and PhD scholarships, almost
all of which demanded rankings), and students receiving grades that
dissatisfied them should have the right to substitute "pass" for the
offending mark. Nothing could better illustrate the foolishness of the
complainants, their jumped-up sense of their own importance, and their
utter Alice-in-Wonderland misunderstanding of just what constituted

graduate study in a university than this memorandum. How extraordinary that such militant ideological buffoonery had brought a proud university to its knees.

The dénouement of the unhappy UBC affair came, as might be expected, in hard-fought struggles in departments, faculty councils, and the university senate. In the end, in October 1995, the proponents of academic freedom and due process managed to triumph over the complaisance and sheep-like timidity of their colleagues, and the Department of Political Science was once again allowed to admit graduate students. The university began, as best it could, to bind up the wounds inflicted on it by its graduate students, some very foolish administrators and faculty, and its president. There seemed little doubt that the most militant feminists had been utterly discredited; at UBC, at least, its faculty alerted to the dangers that unchecked ignorance could cause, they were unlikely ever to do such damage again,[5] although as the dean of arts at the time of the crisis later wrote, "the bitterness remained like an acrid smell across the campus." A good department had been discredited, and its members, even though almost all had done nothing that any sensible human being could consider as worse than a minor error of judgment, would certainly labour under a cloud for years.

In an editorial in September 1995, the *Globe and Mail* put the whole issue very well indeed:

> Someone, somewhere, has to say: "Enough. Your complaints have no merit. We stand by our department and its scholars. We support the curriculum as it stands. We insist on the highest standards in our students, no matter

---

5. Maybe not. The advertisements for UBC's new president, destined to replace the unlamented Strangway, read as if no white males need apply: UBC "welcomes all qualified applicants, especially members of designated employment equity groups." Professor Philip Resnick made this wording a major issue in September 1996, arguing that "this is coded signals.... it's coming pretty close to saying that we want someone from one of these four specific groups as the next university president." Resnick, of course, is precisely correct, notwithstanding the Search Committee chair's rejoinder that only merit will determine the choice (*Globe and Mail*, 12 and 25

what their background. We are doing everything we can to make the university free of real discrimination, but we will not allow the overheated sensitivities of a small minority to stifle freedom of speech on this campus...Everyone is free to challenge [our society's great intellectual] traditions. That is part of what universities are about. But they should do so with facts and reason, not defamation and calumny. If you want to join the battle of ideas at this university, you must first learn to fight by the rules."

Precisely.

If there was any deeper meaning to the UBC affair, it was that many women in the universities (and at least one lawyer, Ms McEwen) believe that all males, especially white males, are an officially suspect category, a group with ingrained sexist and racist prejudices. Their answer clearly is to have more women students in all disciplines, more women faculty, and more women administrators, something difficult to achieve at a time of financial stringency and rapidly declining numbers of tenure-track appointments. Only then will women's concerns be properly dealt with in a truly inclusive university that will remake the world without hierarchy, patriarchy, authority, racism, and sexism. Ideology will remain, of course, but everyone will feel comfortable, and no one will learn anything. What will happen to white male students and faculty in this new post-modernist academic world, given recent experiences, is not pleasant to contemplate, but no one will care if they feel good.

In fact, according to Statistics Canada data, women already

September 1996). As a letter commenting on the controversy noted on 28 September, "if the ad in the paper were to read that anyone can apply, 'especially' white males, how many minorities do you think would bother applying?" UBC seemed unable to break free of its PC albatross.

constitute a majority of all undergraduate students; they received 30.9 percent of all doctoral degrees in 1994–95; and in subjects such as arts and science, education, and fine and applied arts, they were in substantial majorities among those working towards doctorates. In the social sciences, women accounted for 48.2 percent of those studying toward PhDs; in agriculture and biological sciences, 35.4 percent; and in health sciences, 46.8 percent. Only in mathematics, physical sciences, and engineering were women outnumbered decisively by men. That there had been a great disparity in the past between male and female numbers in the professoriate was true; that the corrective process was well under way was also true. In other words, except in a few fields, women made up approximately half of the pool from which the next generation of professors would be drawn.

Statistics Canada's breakdown of the present professoriate was less satisfactory. Of the 27,103 faculty in 1994, women constituted 6433, or 24 percent. The situation was worst at the full professor level — of 11,034 professors, only 1028 were women; but at the assistant professor level, 2249 of 5625 were women. In other words, 40 percent of junior faculty members, the most recently hired, were women. These numbers will likely increase — as equity officers and committees at Canadian universities secure veto or near-veto powers on appointments. At York University, for example, appointments must be cleared through just such a committee, and if a male is recommended for an appointment, the hiring department must be able to demonstrate that the lucky appointee was demonstrably better than any female applicant. Even today, if one excludes the traditional areas (mathematics and engineering) where women have long been underrepresented (but where substantial gains are being made), at least half of the newest faculty in Canada are women.[6]

---

6. It is true that there have been relatively few tenure-track appointments to Canadian universities in the 1990s. In 1970, according to a 1996 study by Edward Renner of Carleton University, there were 360 appointments, of which only 45 went to women. In 1992–93, the last year for which he had broad national data, women received half the posts — but there were only

The situation of female disparity, in other words, is self-correcting. It is simply a matter of time before the doddering heterosexualist white male full professors disappear into retirement; it is only a matter of years before the 50 percent of women assistant professors move up the ranks and take over as chairs of departments, deans of faculties, and presidents of universities. Indeed, it is already happening, for search committees, fearing the wrath of the gender police, beat the bushes with real desperation to find female chairs, deans, and presidents. Sometimes, in their panicky haste, presidential and decanal search committees select the demonstrably unqualified, causing real damage to their institutions. Moreover, in an effort to redress the perceived imbalance in the gender of faculty, the chances of a woman applicant for any tenure-track or tenured post are almost invariably better than those of a male. At UBC, for example, quotas were put in place in 1995 to "guarantee" set percentages of women appointees in the sciences. At first glance, the UBC numbers, where in 1993 women represented 20.5 percent of faculty, support such action — if one can believe, as we do not, that quotas of any kind are ever justifiable in a supposedly meritocratic institution. But those numbers are misleading. Women hold 17.15 percent of tenured appointments and 33 percent of tenure-track appointments. Once the elderly males retire, something certain to occur within a decade at most, women faculty will be close to a majority position at UBC. This same situation is replicated at virtually every university in Canada. Patience is still a virtue, and those who bay for immediate change might benefit from learning to practise it. Under present practices, as A.D. Irvine's thorough study of employment

---

fifty new jobs available. Obviously the dearth of new professorial appointments has increased competition dramatically and made the drive for gender equity a political football. The situation affects men and women alike. A majority of new PhDs in the humanities and social sciences is unlikely to find academic positions, yet the number of doctorates continues to increase and the number of job vacancies continues to decline. In post-Confederation Canadian history, for example, there were three jobs in 1995–96, of which two were in the United States. For an American account of the PhD problem, see Louis Menand, "How to Make a Ph.D. Matter," *New York Times Magazine,* 22 September 1996.

equity in the university demonstrates, if there is discrimination in hiring in the 1990s, "it is more likely to be occurring in favour of, rather than against, women."

Two University of Victoria scholars, James Cutt and Christopher Hodgkinson, wrote that "these are times in some Canadian universities of unreason, immoderation, vengefulness, intolerance, and intimidation, aided and abetted by guilt, insecurity, indifference, opportunism, and ideology." Such cases as those at Western Ontario, UBC, Victoria, UNB, and a dozen other universities across the land are leading politicians and the public to "reflect that universities which have abandoned in substance if not in rhetoric their commitment to quality and fairness, and which are willing to compromise academic freedom on the altar of political correctness and convenience, have undermined their right to autonomy, public regard, generous public funding, and indeed the generosity of private donors." This is the obvious danger, but happily we believe (or, at least, we hope) we can see signs that the silent majority of male and female faculty have been frightened enough by the excesses of reverse discrimination committed in the name of equity to begin to seize back control of their campuses. Fundamentally, the university is not now and never should be a laboratory for trendy social engineering; it is instead a place for research, learning, and scholarship. Where this has been forgotten and where other faddish objectives have instead been put in place, weak and foolish administrators and their ideologically driven faculty demagogues will eventually have much to explain.

Chapter 6

Tenure:
Still a Four-Letter Word?

"TENURE" IS A WORD WITH SEVERAL MEANINGS, a concept with a history — several histories, in fact. Essentially, tenure means possession of an office or a post. It usually refers to public offices, which is where its history began, but it is most often taken to mean academic offices and the grip that professors have on their positions, perquisites, and salaries. In that connection, tenure is thought to be a policy devised to protect academic freedom against undue influence, thereby preserving the university as society's centre of free thought and speech.

Many of those who accept this line of argument also argue that tenure, noble in concept, has been abused. Though endowed with a shining origin, and perhaps once necessary, tenure is now little better than a job-protection device. Worse still, it is a means by which the elderly and incompetent block advancement for the young and meritorious.

Although we do not disagree with this line of argument, we do not find it especially fruitful. Tenure is neither a lustrous beacon of academic freedom nor wholly a job-protection device, a bulwark of protection against generational incompetence. Like most human contrivances, it is somewhere in between. It started off as job security. Academics had tenure long before there was academic freedom. And academics were not alone. Most public offices over time have been populated by the long-serving and the self-serving. The two are not necessarily the same, but they often are.

That is why, in the nineteenth century, the public insisted on implementing the idea of appointment and promotion by merit. Merit was determined by competitive examination. By today's standards these examinations were imperfect, but at the time they were far better than the spoils system they replaced.

Most academic jobs in Canada were, as in many other places, effectively civil service jobs. Those that were not were religious, and the churches had their own civil service traditions in which the merit principle was supplemented by the faith principle; as a result, conflicts over ideas were more frequent in religious colleges. Few civil servants were ever fired, as long as they kept their heads down and their hands clean; the same was true of professors.

There were occasional eruptions, but the remarkable fact is not that people were occasionally fired for professing the wrong belief, but how few actually "merited" firing. Professors had a certain freedom of speech and a certain liberty of inquiry, but within the limits generally set by society. Only the brave and the foolhardy stepped outside the bounds of conformity. In the meantime the professoriate, like other civil servants, accepted and imposed the merit principle on itself. It was based on competitive examination, which by the 1940s had come to mean the possession of a PhD. Later, as numbers increased, it came to mean the PhD plus — articles, a book, two books, many books, and so forth.

Of course, like other parts of the civil service, and like any large organization, the university floated on a cushion of temporary labour — apprentices who had not yet proved their merit according to the often flexible standards of their employers. Such people could be, and were, frequently traded around and sometimes discouraged altogether. This was often the case with women, for the universities, like almost every other large organization in society, were a male bastion. But then, given the times, relatively few women wanted the academic life.

The appearance of tenure in its modern guise in the 1950s actually made little difference to the way academics lived their lives. Most were not conscious that they needed extra protection for their freedom of thought or speech, and most did not need it. So tenure, as protection,

was easy to concede for university administrations — it made no difference — and easy to accept for academics.

Moreover, tenure coincided with the increasing professionalization of the professoriate. As professors grew in numbers, they wanted
to grow in status too. Tenure was convenient. It was a sign of quality
control, and the quality examined was not the need for protected speech
but academic merit. Since universities were bureaucracies, and as individual opinion was a difficult thing to justify or defend, the acquisition
of tenure essentially became a quantitative process. It is, still.

Professors do not, on the whole, project radical ideas, or if they do,
it is because radicalism is the trend of the times. Professors as a group
are a timid lot, not because they are demoralized, but because they are
like other sectors of society, and because, institutionally, they still reflect
their civil service origins.

What, then, are we to make of tenure? Stripped of its sacred
mythology, tenure in its origins is not very different from what until
recently was a general pattern of civil service job security. Tenure is not
unique, in other words. Indeed, many people have tenure — judges in
most countries, or Canadian senators, or members of the House of
Lords. But when the word comes up, it usually refers to the employment of professional academics. Academics, it is true, don't have quite
the security of Supreme Court judges or British peers, who wait until
age seventy-five or death separates them from their posts. In Canada,
though not in Quebec, professors usually retire at sixty-five. But until
then, in normal circumstances, what they have, they hold.

There are many ways of looking at this phenomenon. There is the
financial approach. In Canadian universities, salaries ordinarily make
up at least 80 percent of budgets. In contemplating university finances,
this 80 percent is a heavy, intractable weight.

Then there is the generational approach. Dr Wayne Roberts, a
left-wing historian and journalist without a university post, wrote
in Toronto's *Now* newspaper that tenure had created "a gerontocracy
that allowed second-raters to order graduate students to follow conventional studies, then fill a string of one-year appointments while

full-timers are on sabbatical." To Roberts, those "who do the bull work of academic teaching and publishing enjoy no job security, while those on tenure...lord it over them." Overtones of an oppressed proletariat at the mercy of the brutal bosses aside, a similarly bleak view is certainly widespread in industry. The report of a Conference Board of Canada/Natural Sciences and Engineering Research Council of Canada conference on University-Industry Research & Development collaboration in 1995 indicates that industry participants demanded the abolition of tenure.

Right-wing politicians say the same. When his successful campaign for the Ontario premiership was in full flight in 1995, Progressive Conservative Mike Harris said bluntly: "The tenured system as it exists today...is passé, is gone. ...I don't think tenure makes sense today." Harris' government and his Common Sense Revolution have often seemed to be harshness personified, but on this issue he probably had caught the public mood: academics are freeloaders protected by tenure.[1]

Harris and the Conference Board are mostly right. And so, mostly, is Roberts. In some respects, they don't go far enough. The basic argument for tenure regularly proclaimed by academics and their organizations — tenure to protect freedom of thought — does not work as advertised. No more than anyone else, professors do not like to read or hear things they disagree with. As a result, universities are mostly distinguished by uniformity rather than diversity of thought.

One litmus test would be the first sentence of the last paragraph, "Harris and the Conference Board are mostly right." It will not be taken as a signal for the academy to ponder the proposition, for the academy has already made up its collective mind on that score, and

---

1. The *Ottawa Citizen* on 8 May 1995 denounced Harris for this comment: "There's no factual basis for Harris's assertion that tenured professors can coast for 25 years on past performance," it wrote. "All universities put their teaching staff through rigorous annual productivity reviews. ...all universities have the right to fire incompetent faculty." The first statement is simply untrue; the second is correct, but exercised only in the rarest of circumstances.

TENURE

the signal has already gone out for the herd to gather and bellow, turning its most insensitive parts outward, to face the approaching danger. The noise will be substantial; the sense, less so.

Of course, there are those who agree with us. University of Toronto historian Michael Bliss noted that the "concept of tenure [is] so offensive that we should find ways to do away with it." His colleague Edward Shorter added that tenure "is really a system of featherbedding for a whole generation of academics who were hired in the 1960s... many have not worked out...yet they are protected by tenure to the detriment" of the university. And the Canadian Association of University Business Officers has denounced the "deadwood" cluttering the university and remarked that "angry taxpayers are demanding to know why professors should enjoy virtual lifetime security...tenure is an outmoded system that all too often serves to protect the mediocre and incompetent." (We generally agree with CAUBO's sentiments — but we have never been overly impressed by the business efficiency of universities. However, business officers usually do *not* have tenure.)

Large numbers of faculty do work very hard, and many have worked out well. But, in our view, there can be no doubt that the universities have far too many professors who do little but meet their classes, teach in a desultory way, sit on a committee or two, and do no research or writing. These are the faculty who are on permanent internal sabbatical. Indeed, given the aging professoriate of the mid-1990s and the effects of boredom on productivity, such indolence is probably even more prevalent than it was in the mid-1980s when we published *The Great Brain Robbery.* And there is no sign that university administrators are any more willing to fight the faculty associations and to try to challenge the tenured layabouts than they were in 1984.

Nothing ever stays the same, however, and academic freedom is under attack in 1990s Canada as never before. In 1984, political correctness in Canada was just a small cloud in a large blue sky. No one could have believed that equity offices, speech codes, and sexual harassment officers would become powerful influences on university teachers and their employers. No one could have believed that an obscure psychology professor, writing on racial differences, would provoke a provincial premier to demand that his university fire him. No one would have thought it credible that an article on date rape in a student university newspaper by an assistant professor of mathematics would stir up a national debate and lead to his forced resignation. No one would have conceived it possible that graduate students at a major university would charge that a "chilly climate" offended them — and that the university administration would leap to their bidding to bar a whole department from taking new graduate students. The world of the university has changed dramatically, and zealotry threatens academic freedom today.

Whatever its origins, tenure today is loudly proclaimed as a device to protect academic freedom. At the very least, we must look at the issue once more in the light of changed circumstances.

———————

What is tenure? According to "University Tenured Appointments and Their Purpose," a statement by the Canadian Association of University Teachers (CAUT), tenure is "the category of continuing, permanent appointment held by a member of the academic staff following successful completion of a probationary period." After this period of assessment, usually from four to seven years, the professor is assessed, with varying degrees of rigour depending on the university, usually by a department committee, then by a dean's committee, and finally by a university-wide committee. The university's president then signs off on the decision for or against a permanent appointment, occasionally overturning it to grant or to deny tenure. Once granted tenure, a professor then can only be asked to leave the university in carefully defined circumstances. But if he or she is denied tenure, the faculty member is obliged to depart the university almost immediately.

Ordinarily in making their decisions, tenure committees assess teaching, scholarship, and service to the university and the community. This review will usually, but not always, involve student and collegial assessments of teaching, appraisals of the candidate's published scholarship by experts inside and outside the university, and letters from those who have served on committees with the tenure seeker. At some universities, the applicant must be judged "excellent" in at least one of these three areas; at others, "high competence" is required in all three, if excellence is not found in any one area; some simply pass a judgment based on turning a blind eye to the lack of evidence. As that suggests, all such judgments are by definition arbitrary, and what one assessor might believe is excellent teaching, another may consider weak. Student judgments of teaching, in addition, sometimes praise showmanship more than intellectual content; nonetheless, more and more universities these days feel obliged to give the "customers" an increasing say in tenure decisions and in many other areas of academic life, ranging from seats on the board of governors to the content of programs and to the purchase of engineering laboratory equipment. Naturally enough, at some institutions and in some departments, the award of tenured status is a joke, a hurdle to be cleared while colleagues carefully lower the bar to ground level. At better universities, however, the process can be long and arduous; at such universities, moreover, more weight in tenure decisions is given to published scholarship.

Although we are not great supporters of the idea of tenure, we have no doubt that if it is to exist at all, it should be based primarily on the assessment of publications and research. We do not believe that pages published should be totted up and tenure awarded for exceeding the Stakhanovite norm. The quality of the work is all important. We would go so far as to say that there can be no great teaching if a professor is not immersed in research. The search for new scientific discoveries, for new mathematical solutions, for archivally based historical interpretations — that is what universities exist to do. A university is not a continuation of high school; it is a research institution dedicated to the advancement of knowledge, and those who do not contribute to this end ought not to be employed there. The best teachers we had as students, the best teachers among our colleagues today, were and are those whose lives are consumed by their research and who can communicate their excitement and their enthusiasm about grappling with research-based questions to their classes.[2] This does not mean that the publication of unreadable, pointless "research" is either important or desirable.

If Canada had a system that declared some universities as "research" institutions and others as "boutique" or teaching universities, then a more rational system for deciding tenure could be put in place. A teaching university would reward good teachers; a research university would tenure its best researchers. But Canadians who pretend that all provinces are equal also pretend that all universities are equal. The provinces finance them at the same rate per student and, as a result, everyone pays lip-service to the three-track system of awarding tenure. This inclusiveness makes for a fundamentally dishonest system.

Still, the three tracks of research, teaching, and service are held up as sacred writ in deciding tenure, and, recently, thanks to attacks in the legislatures and to a tendency to give too much weight to student opinion, the assessment of teaching has increasingly come to be pronounced the most important component of the road that leads to tenure. We do not think this tendency makes sense; indeed, we think that if it proceeds further, it will weaken Canadian universities even more, ensure that they become truly mediocre and brain dead, and likely drive out the best researching faculty, the only ones with international and national reputations. Fortunately, perhaps, salary decisions — where there is any flexibility left in the granting of pay raises — almost always reward the productive publishing scholars.

Good young scholars are aware of the difficulties of the tenure-track system. Consider the comments of Mary McDonald Pavelka, an

---

2. It is, of course, difficult to measure the effectiveness of teachers, let alone to compare the success as teachers of those who publish and those who do not. The research studies that try to make this assessment often seem to produce conflicting results, but one summary study noted that "teachers disdaining publishing because of their affirmation of commitment to teaching as a full-time enterprise appear no better nor no worse teachers than do the publishers." Realistically, the "Ten Commandments of Tenure Success," as defined Marcia Lynn Whicker et al., in *Getting Tenure* (London 1993), have as Number 1: "Publish, publish, publish!"

anthropologist at the University of Calgary, who talked to the *Calgary Herald* in 1994 about getting tenure. "The hoops you have to jump through to get it are endless," she said, not least the very long ten years of post-secondary education and five years of probationary teaching. During those five years, Pavelka added, "you must excel in three areas — research, administration and teaching. It's a heavy load. You have to demonstrate an ability to generate and disseminate new knowledge." Tenure, she says, doesn't end the work: it "only guarantees that you get to continue jumping through the hoops. Once you get tenure, the pace, the demands increase. The university expects more of you. Now I teach thousands of students. I have to publish every single year and I have to carry a very heavy administrative load." All this work initially pays around $45,000 a year.

We are prepared to accept that everything is as Pavelka described it — for her. We do not believe that the system is as rigorous or demanding for most faculty in most universities. Nor do we complacently accept the claims of long working hours made by professors. Michael Keefer's generally sensible *Lunar Perspectives: Field Notes from the Culture Wars* reports on a 1992 study commissioned by two organizations of Canadian professors of English that suggests an average professorial work week of 57 hours — including 8 hours in class, 17 or 18 hours of correcting papers, 3.5 hours of supervising MA and PhD students, 3.5 hours of professional work, and 7 hours of committee-type work; the remaining time presumably is spent in research and writing, reading for classes, lecture preparation, and the like. If accurate, this survey reveals a hard-working professoriate. The flaw, however, is that the survey is not based on empirical observation but on self-completed questionnaires, and its validity is dubious. Some professors do work hard, but many do not, especially those who have tenure.

Of course, a large and increasing number of those teaching in the universities do not have tenure and have little hope of ever achieving it. *Maclean's* 1995 figures show that at some universities, the bulk of the teaching is by untenured faculty, much of it almost certainly by sessional appointees who are ineligible for tenure. Queen's University, always at or near the top of the overall rankings, for example, teaches only 41 percent of its first-year classes with tenured faculty; McMaster, among the medical/doctoral universities, by contrast, covers 76 percent of its classes this way. Among comprehensive universities, 87 percent of York University's classes are taught by the tenured, while at Simon Fraser University only 31.6 percent are. And among the primarily undergraduate institutions, the range is similarly varied. St Francis Xavier University students have 87 percent of their first-year classes taught by tenured faculty; Wilfrid Laurier University's students in first year have only 41 percent so taught. What this suggests is that the tenured faculty prefer, wherever they can manage it, to teach smaller classes of graduate students or upper-level courses rather than the sometimes very large first-year classes. As the first year, the year that filters out most of those who will not complete their degrees, is arguably the most important for students, it surely should have the best teachers instructing. But perhaps the best teachers are not among the tenured?

Whatever the rigour of the tenuring process, virtually every single tenure-track academic — more than 95 percent certainly — become tenured at the end of the probationary period. Most earn their tenure through hard work and deserve it, though there is unfortunately no guarantee whatsoever that the diligence that preceded tenure will be matched by equivalent effort after its granting. But there are many dubious cases.

Academics, like most other groups, have a tendency to become attached to those with whom they work. It is difficult to tell a colleague, Professor Jones, that she will be let go at the end of this year. To be sure, Jones has published nothing, her teaching is dreadful, and she failed to turn up for any of the Department Curriculum Committee meetings. Even so, everyone likes her, especially the chair. Moreover, the hiring committee members who chose her five years before have a vested interest in seeing their judgment confirmed. Jones was better than Smith and Brown in 1990, and to prove this point we must give her tenure in 1995. As Steven Cahn noted of the United States: "Without doubt most colleges and universities have awarded tenure too liberally.

Instead of individuals being required to demonstrate why they deserve tenure, a school has been expected to demonstrate why they don't."

The result of such decisions, good or bad, is that most faculty in Canadian universities have tenure. At the University of Calgary in 1994, 950 of the university's approximately 1300 teaching staff had tenured appointments; at the University of Alberta in Edmonton, 1343 of 1669 professors were tenured. There are no Canada-wide data, but of the 27,103 professors in Canada, according to CAUT's data for 1994, 74.6 percent are full and associate professors and, therefore, almost certainly tenured. More to the point, almost all of the remaining 6310 faculty at every university in Canada will secure tenure in the normal course of events, the current budgetary crises affecting every province and every university notwithstanding.[3]

Once granted, tenure implies that the appointment can be terminated only for appropriate reasons and after fair procedures have been followed. And the appropriate reasons? The University of Manitoba collective agreement says that "a Faculty member may be suspended with loss of pay or dismissed for just and reasonable cause, for example, but without limiting the generality of the foregoing, for persistent neglect of duty, incompetence or gross misconduct." Moreover, virtually all collective agreements now include (or will certainly do so after their next renegotiation) a clause covering "financial exigency," the situation that would result from a university being in such serious financial difficulties that its only way out is to lay off large numbers, and conceivably whole departments, of its faculty. What it all amounts to is that once Professor Jones has been granted tenure, if she doesn't steal

---

3. Paula Caplan, *Lifting a Ton of Feathers: A Woman's Guide to Surviving in the Academic World* (Toronto 1994), says flatly that "although white women and ethnic minority women and men are being hired in academia more frequently than in previous eras, white men are still the most likely to receive tenure." She cites one 1992 U.S. study as evidence, a dangerously thin basis for a disgraceful and sweeping generalization that many will find deeply offensive with its implications of sexism and racism. Our experience (again a thin generalization, but one we at least acknowledge) has been that women and ethnic minorities are, if anything, more likely to receive tenure than white males. But then, as we argue, virtually everyone gets tenure.

the department's petty cash or seduce students too brazenly, and the university avoids bankruptcy, she has her job for life. Financial exigency clauses, which exist in every collective agreement, have in the past seemed a remote possibility. But provincial debt, the drying up of federal transfer payments, and widespread public dissatisfaction with universities have created the possibility that they may occur. We believe that financial exigency clauses will be much less likely to be needed if the universities could be persuaded to do their jobs sensibly and to police themselves.

Common sense tells us that in any large group of people, in any job, there will be the very small percentage of superstars, a larger group of those of above-average competence, a very large group of the competent, and a small number of utter incompetents. The universities are no different in this respect than the British Columbia public service, the judiciary, or General Motors, all organizations with their own forms of tenure. Public servants used to be guaranteed their jobs in much the same way as professors, until debt and deficits led federal, provincial, and municipal governments to begin cutting back. Judges have lifetime tenure to ensure that they are not pressured by fear of removal into making decisions for the wrong reasons. And many corporations, even if they do not admit to it, have a form of tenure in their collective agreements for unionized workers or by tacit understanding for their management personnel.

Faculty associations and the provincial and national associations argue that the process for the award of tenure is long and rigorous, so much so that, once granted, serious appraisal need never be undertaken again. As we have suggested, sometimes the process is severe, and sometimes it isn't. CAUT also maintains that tenure can be removed wherever incompetence or misconduct is found. True enough, every faculty union contract says so, but how many tenured faculty have been let go in Canada in the last decade? There were more than 27,000 university professors in 1994, but our best guesstimate is that no more than fifteen tenured faculty have been fired over the years 1984–94, a number that surely underestimates the number of incompetents in any group of that size. True, some professors, when faced with a hearing designed to strip them of their tenure, choose to leave quietly to find another line of work. But in our combined eighty years of teaching in three different universities, together with hearsay from every university in the land, we have heard of no more than twenty such cases. Does CAUT have any hard evidence of substantial numbers fleeing the tenure-stripping process across Canada? We think not.

The blame for this situation can properly be placed on faculty associations and university administrations equally. No matter how obvious the academic incompetence, the faculty association can almost always be counted on to defend Professor Worthless to the limit; to employ expensive law firms; to drag out hearings; to cost the university more in time, money, and negative publicity than can be readily borne. In the circumstances, administrations ordinarily are reluctant to take on the task of ridding their campuses of their faculty dullards. Such tolerance makes a mockery of the university's stated goals. The result, even if the theory is different, is that job security for all practical purposes is absolute.

Of course, incompetence is difficult to prove, usually because a conspiracy of silence protects likely candidates. CAUT always argues that "the fact that professors continue to be subject to regular evaluation throughout their working careers" guarantees that tenure is not a protection for the slothful or the brain-dead. Sometimes, and at some universities, this is so. Every university looks at its professors' research, teaching, and service when promotion from assistant to associate professor and from associate to full professor is considered. The first such appraisal ordinarily coincides with a decision on tenure, the second comes several years after its grant. The quality of the appraisal varies depending on the university, and, since there are large numbers of faculty who seem satisfied to remain as career associate professors, many academics never face this second scrutiny. In any case, even if promotion is denied, there is no sanction; not even salary is affected — most universities have salary floors, but not ceilings.

But surely every university assesses its faculty's work each year?

Some do, most notably in Alberta. The University of Calgary has a system that rates each professor each year on teaching, research, and service in determining merit pay. A zero-merit increment for two years running requires that a case be made why the faculty member should not be dismissed. Dismissal rarely results, however, though early retirement packages may well be taken by those who feel the heat. This system is a good one, which likely explains why it is followed in so few institutions! At York University in Toronto, for example, the only time faculty are obliged to report on their year's work is when they return from sabbatical, and this perfunctory account usually takes the form of a "Hi, I'm back" letter to the dean. In such circumstances, how could a chair or dean know what all faculty members are doing? York is by no means unique; indeed, it is closer to the norm than Calgary. CAUT's claim of rigorous, ongoing evaluation is simply untrue in most Canadian universities.

The only way to change this reality is for the provincial governments and the university administrations to accept the fact that the professoriate will not police its own ranks. As a result, presidents and deans must gird their loins and actively take up the management of their faculty, if necessary with the prod of provincial penalties to spur them on. There must be regular and meaningful reporting by faculty of their work, even if this means changing university union contracts. There must be a willingness by administrations to get tough with those who simply fail to do the job they are paid for — and that includes those faculty who abuse the universities' facilities to set themselves up as consultants without even a shadow of oversight. The provincial governments must make the universities police themselves.

There is one recent example of a university acting to clean house. At St Michael's College of the University of Toronto a "dishonest and untrustworthy" professor who ran a publishing/teaching empire in the United States and the Caribbean, who misused sick leave, and who generally did not appear to take his teaching seriously was forced out after a long, $500,000 hearing in 1994 in which all the members of the arbitration panel, including the professor's own nominee, agreed on dismissal. One commentator, Professor John Scott Cowan of the University of Ottawa, said, "the University of Toronto should really be congratulated for taking action on this matter. It would have been just as easy for them to let him quietly retire." To its eternal credit — and to its shame that it took so long to act — the St. Michael's administration laid down a marker and set a valuable precedent, "pour encourager les autres." Once it goes beyond a certain point, misconduct will no longer be tolerated at Toronto.

CAUT would not — could not — disagree with this decision. Misconduct is grounds for removing a professor's tenure, and due process had been followed. The fact that the dismissed professor was making huge sums of money also probably let CAUT go along with the decision; envy of the successful is a well-known academic trait. Of course, as professors always say with their eyes cast heavenward, job security is not now and never has been the reason for tenure.

Instead, CAUT maintains, "the most important reason for the security of employment which is called tenure is to ensure academic freedom." Academic freedom is defined as follows: "The freedom enjoyed by the academic staff to teach and conduct research without hindrance from persons or groups inside or outside the university," so that "society will have the benefit of honest judgment and independent criticism which might be withheld because of fear of offending a dominant social group or transient social attitude." CAUT then quotes Canadian historian Frank Underhill that the academic's responsibility is "to seek new knowledge and understanding about nature and society, and to keep asking questions, often very embarrassing ones, about established beliefs and conventional wisdom."

It goes without saying that the very large numbers of unionized faculty in Canada have their academic freedom protected in the collective agreements reached between their university administrations and their faculty associations. At York University, for example, which has been operating under a collective agreement for two decades, the contract notes that "the parties agree to continue their practice of upholding, protecting, and promoting academic freedom as essential to the pursuit of truth and the fulfilment of the University's objectives." The York contract also explicitly protects the rights of faculty "to criticize the University or society at large" and "to be free from institutional censorship." The University of British Columbia, the site of the most appalling recent violation of academic freedom in Canada, also has a policy on academic freedom which ends with these ringing phrases: "Behaviour which obstructs free and full discussion, not only of ideas which are safe and accepted, but of those which may be unpopular or even abhorrent, vitally threatens the University's forum. Such behaviour cannot be tolerated."

Academic freedom, however, is not licence. It does not extend to defaming individuals or to calling for the overthrow of government. Nor does it include a professor's right to teach whatever he or she wishes. Courses must be authorized, but the way the material is taught is properly a matter of individual concern.

We believe absolutely in academic freedom. We accept York and UBC's statement, CAUT's definition, Underhill's statement, and the contract language used across the land. We believe that it is always useful to challenge ideas, even those that may be treasured or those that are pernicious. The problem is that many university administrations and professors do not appear to agree with the concept any more than politicians and the public do. UBC's statement clearly failed to protect the political science professors who were accused after 1992 of various "crimes," and the UBC faculty, taken as a whole, failed to support its political science colleagues. Even CAUT has been less than fervent in its defence of academic freedom on occasion, and some groups within CAUT, most especially its Status of Women Committee, have seemed particularly hostile to anyone and any organization that might disagree with its diagnosis of the problems of the university and society.

It used to be, as historian Michiel Horn noted in 1996, that the "enemies of academic freedom have been identifiably Conservative in their politics." This, however, is no longer so. Today, the enemies of academic freedom are more likely to be found on the left, not least among the proponents of feminism, Marxism, and multiculturalism or among those who wish to prevent any manifestation of anti-religious or sexist discussion or any research on race. Today, the most vigorous defence of academic freedom has rested with groups such as the Society for Academic Freedom and Scholarship, usually thought to be on the right, and the occasional university administration. To his credit, Horn acknowledges that, in the 1990s, the enemies of academic freedom have been "more conspicuous within the university than outside it. There are some (faculty, students, administrators) who are striving for the achievement within the academy of a culture of comfort, from which ideas they find disturbing and offensive will be excluded." Even CAUT itself notes that "academic freedom must now be protected against the carelessness or wilfulness of peers." Exactly. The greatest threat to academic freedom now comes from within our ideologically blinkered universities. As hinted above, it needs to be said loudly and clearly that in the universities, and especially in the humanities and social sciences, the received wisdom is strongly Marxist, multiculturalist, and feminist, and often a combination of the three.

Horn defends academic freedom by observing that if it did not exist and if it were not protected by tenure, then "only the independently wealthy or those unconcerned about their financial and professional prospects would be able to pursue research...to challenge established authority, or to offer economic, social, political or other comment or advice that may prove unwelcome." This view is echoed by Donald Savage of CAUT, who argues that "those who attack tenure ...really want...a subservient and acquiescent university community which will obsequiously uphold the status quo." Another supporter of tenure, Edward Monahan, noted that "university faculty have an obligation to work on the frontiers of knowledge" and, in so doing, face the risk that they will encounter opposition when the results of their inquiries are reported. We concede that there are always people, governments, corporations, and groups within and without the walls of academe who will try to throttle free inquiry.

For our part, however, even with tenure and guaranteed academic freedom, we see very few scholars who are willing to challenge conventional attitudes. In the first place, most academics write very little, and the great bulk of publication is undertaken by a small group — say 10 percent of the professoriate — of prolific scholars. The remaining professors may publish a single book in their academic lifetime or, more likely, a few articles and book reviews; many never do any serious research at all or, if they do, never publish a single line. (There is no thorough Canadian study of just who publishes high-quality or undistinguished work in quantity and who does not.) Most academics, naturally enough, just like most citizens, support the status quo in society and in their university, and the idea of even those few publishing scholars ever writing something that flies in the face of conventional wisdom is all but inconceivable. All faculty teach, but many lectures and seminars are dry recitations of fact and non-judgmental assessments of differing viewpoints. Many entire subject areas (in medicine, engineering, pharmacy, science, and mathematics, for example) aim at teaching a corpus of knowledge rather than setting out differing or challenging viewpoints. In other words, in only a few areas — psychology, sociology, political science, or history, for example — are issues likely to be raised that might provoke outrage.

If a scholar writes an assessment of medieval armour, to cite an example, who could be incensed, other than an expert in gorget plates who disagrees with the account of how metal forgers worked in Aquitaine? But if a historian says that the Holocaust did not occur, or that the Croats slaughtered thousands of Serbs in the Second World War, or that large numbers of Lithuanians were members of Hitler's SS, controversy is certain to erupt. If a psychologist says that Asians have higher intelligence than whites or blacks, university walls may tremble. Some subjects, some issues, are certain to challenge conventional wisdom and social attitudes.

But by definition — and by choice — very few scholars work in these areas. It is clearly much safer to research and write on medieval armour than on racial differences. And even in hotly contested subject areas, it is much more common for practitioners to support the status quo than to threaten it. The odds, after all, are not bad that the status quo and the received version more often than not are both better and more correct than the still unknown. Professors are human, and most do not thrive on high-stress controversies. As Professor Trevor Hodge noted, "the right to speak freely would be greatly served if more professors actually did it." But, he went on, "saying something genuinely unpopular and controversial" would be a different matter: "in such a case the vaunted protection of tenure is a puny thing." If he had written in the *Globe and Mail* that blacks were congenitally stupid or that most rape victims had been asking for it, he said, "I do not think tenure could save me from the wrath to come." That is an extreme example, but Hodge noted that even on less controversial subjects, professors are ordinarily unwilling to speak out, bound as they are in defensive silence by the "omerta of the Mafia."

In the circumstances, is tenure for all necessary to protect the academic freedom of a tiny minority? For the unionized faculty — a group that includes faculty in Quebec, most Atlantic Canada universities (including Memorial, Mount Allison, and New Brunswick), most of the Ontario universities (Toronto and Western Ontario being the major exceptions), and all the Manitoba and Saskatchewan universities — the protection afforded by their collective agreements' guarantee of academic freedom surely renders tenure unnecessary. CAUT agrees that academic freedom has been given "a firm legal basis" in collective agreements, but it says nothing about why tenure should still be necessary in the light of explicit contractual guarantees of academic freedom.

Many universities, especially in British Columbia and Alberta where university faculty are denied union status by provincial edicts, are not unionized, however. Yet even their outspoken faculty do not need tenure to protect their academic freedom. First, academic freedom is protected by the Anglo-American-Canadian tradition of what James O'Toole called "the long-nurtured societal judgment of what is a just, fair, and effective mode of education in a democracy." Then, every university in Canada, unionized or not, has a statement of academic freedom that proclaims its faculty's right to write, research, and speak out. Every province has a human rights commission devoted to protecting people's rights to speak freely. And virtually every faculty association belongs to CAUT, which monitors threats to academic freedom and is free to call for the censure of any university that violates it.

There is, moreover, the Canadian Charter of Rights and Freedoms, which aims to protect Canadians' rights to free speech. Doesn't every Canadian have a guaranteed right to freedom of speech? Everyone thought so, until a Supreme Court of Canada decision upholding the concept of mandatory retirement in Ontario and British Columbia universities in December 1990 stated that the Charter did not apply to universities as employers: "The Charter was not intended to cover activities by non-governmental entities created by government for legally facilitating private individuals to do things of their own choosing." The majority decision also noted that "the preservation of academic freedom is a matter of pressing and substantial importance... academic freedom and excellence is necessary to our continuance as a lively democracy." The universities, in the view of the learned justices who may not have been in the universities for some years, are "centres of excellence on the cutting edge of new discoveries and ideas," and it is tenure's protection of academic freedom that makes them so.

This decision has been used by CAUT's presidents, its executive director, and others to argue that because the Charter in no way applies to universities, tenure is the only defence of academic freedom. We do not agree. The mandatory retirement case was not about tenure or academic freedom. It dealt with the age at which faculty must retire in those universities that had not put other regimes in place in their collective agreements. In other words, the central issue of the protection of academic freedom and its connection to tenure was not directly confronted by the Court, whatever its decision may have said in passing. Moreover, Mme Justice Bertha Wilson, in her dissent, disagreed strongly that the Charter did not apply to universities. Who knows what a future judgment in a different legal context on the applicability of the Charter of Rights and Freedoms to the universities might say? Wilson's dissents in other areas have frequently pointed the way to the future, for good or ill. In other words, until the Charter's protection, or not, of academic freedom is directly tested, the matter remains open, CAUT notwithstanding.[4]

The CAUT position is again less than straightforward when the only growing segment of the teaching staff at Canadian (and American) universities, sessional appointments, is considered. The professoriate presently consists of the tenured faculty, the tenure-stream faculty who are on track to being assessed for tenure, the part-time faculty who teach a single course for a few thousand dollars a year because that is all they can get or it is what they prefer, and the sessionals. These "marginal academics," as sessional faculty have been called, are hired to teach for a year or sometimes two, very often for pathetically low salaries (often as low as $5000 to $8000 a two-term course), and they can only rarely make their way onto the tenure track. In 1996 there were said to be 25,000 sessional and part-time teachers in Ontario universities alone, a number at least doubled when the rest of the country is added in. The professor of English at a New York college who wrote to the *New York Times* that ten retirees in his department had been replaced by adjunct (or sessional) professors hired at a far lower cost than if his institution had recruited tenure-track professors was not speaking of a situation unique to his college or country.

CAUT has nominal sympathy for those stuck in this trap, but it is always overridden by the fear that widespread use of sessionals threatens an end-run around permanent appointments by allowing universities to service their students at a much lower cost than if they used tenured and tenure-track faculty. Job security, in other words, rears its ugly head. CAUT, however, does add that sessionals and part-timers do not often benefit from the protection of academic freedom in university

---

4. In early 1997 the Supreme Court in the *Carosella* decision, a case involving the destruction of documents by a rape crisis centre, appeared to reverse its position that institutions with public funding were not subject to the Charter. "They have said universities are not government actors," one of those involved in the case said. "How can they now turn around?" Very easily. At the very least, the CAUT position that the Charter is no protector of academic freedom has been savaged.

contracts. As historian Michael Bliss observed, the sessional appointees are often intellectually more venturesome than their seniors, but get few of the protections supposedly offered by tenure. "It's as though society were to offer a guaranteed annual income for everyone but the poor."

The plight of the sessionals — PhDs who have been unable to find full-time, tenure-track teaching posts — is a serious one. They are entitled to every bit as much academic freedom as a tenured professor, and they are deserving of a job, especially as many of them are better teachers and more published than some of their nominal superiors who hold tenured positions and draw high salaries. This situation is indefensible at the best of times, and the 1990s are not the best of times. Indeed, CAUT's instinctive response to see the sessionals as a threat to job security for its members expresses what is most wrong with academe: selfishness combined with political shortsightedness. Without tenure, the ineffective among the professoriate could be replaced by the best of the newly minted PhDs.

We might also note that some universities — Toronto's York, for one, until the administration in August 1996 took advantage of the lapsing of the faculty association's contract and unilaterally revoked the contract clauses — give faculty the right to teach after the mandatory retirement age of sixty-five. In Quebec, where there is no mandatory retirement, some faculty stay on forever. One McGill professor, for example, is seventy-seven — and under provincial law he is paid his pension *and* his salary until the day he finally decides to totter off. The implications of this policy are serious indeed. The older faculty are, by definition, the highest paid, and the cadre of professors in their sixties eats up a huge percentage of the university budget. Moreover, every professor who remains on staff after sixty-five denies a post to one, or, given the salary disparity, even two or three young scholars. This is no exaggeration: a senior full professor in Arts may well expect to receive $100,000 a year or more, and approximately 14 percent in fringe benefits; faculty in professional faculties and in some disciplines like economics routinely earn much more. A tenure-track junior assistant professor, however, starts at a salary of approximately $38,000 in most universities.

What is needed is some method to encourage an orderly flow of faculty out of, and into, the university system. The thousands of expensively educated PhDs, many people of genuine promise who cannot find a university job in this era of cutbacks, wait on the professoriate, the universities, and the provinces to act. They may well wait forever.

The answer to this systemic failure is to eliminate tenure as job security. As we do, Professor Michiel Horn has argued that tenure came into being in its present form to create secure employment for highly trained professionals, not to protect academic freedom. In essence, however, the origins are immaterial for, today, tenure equals job security, and it should not.

We believe in academic freedom and insist that it be preserved, protected, and fought for wherever it may be challenged. In our view, tenure is unnecessary to protect academic freedom in the unionized universities, and we believe it is unnecessary in the non-unionized ones, too. When Philippe Rushton's ouster from the University of Western Ontario was demanded by Premier David Peterson because of his writings on racial differences, the university refused to comply. Western is not unionized, and its administration deemed that its statement of academic freedom was just as binding as if it was. If some universities do not have tough academic freedom codes, they should draft them forthwith to defend their faculty against increasingly intrusive provincial governments and politically correct non-governmental organizations.

Instead of tenured jobs without term, what might be more productive for the health of the university system are renewable contracts running for five to seven years, with genuine annual reporting and monitoring of research accomplished and of the quality of teaching, a position advocated by the minister of education in Ontario and the Ontario Undergraduate Student Alliance. At the end of a prescribed period, the faculty member would be assessed and a decision made on renewal. One Columbia University professor, David Helfand, refused tenure and, instead, negotiated a renewable fixed-term contract with his university. In the third year of the five-year contract, the administration agreed to appoint a faculty committee to review Helfand's teaching, scholarship, and service and to make a recommendation for or against renewal. He is now approaching his third such review. As he noted, assistant professors undergo serious reviews of their work before they get tenure. "Why, if it is useful for a 35-year-old, untenured professor to summarize his or her accomplishments and future plans and submit them to review by peers, is it anathema for a faculty member [with tenure] to do the same? Why is it never appropriate to end the tenure of someone over the age of 40?"

Just as the vast majority of faculty get tenure now, so, we expect, would most faculty secure their renewals under the Helfand system. But the university administrations would be able — with due process and with evidence — to clean house of those who persistently have done no research or have taught badly for the last half-decade. The CAUT presidents who maintain that there is continual assessment of faculty under the tenure system should not object.

They do, however. It is CAUT's position that "formal, regular review of the entitlement of faculty members to continue in tenured appointments is unnecessary... There would be little benefit to the universities or to the general public if performance were also reviewed at five or six year intervals... Periodic review... would distort individual research schedules to the detriment of the advancement of knowledge. There would be a tendency to cycle research and scholarship into the arbitrary time period fixed by the review period." The president of the Ontario Confederation of University Faculty Associations (OCUFA), Michael Piva, agrees, arguing that "university professors are already reviewed more vigorously than any other profession that I'm aware of." Which is to say, not at all.

These are self-serving statements uttered by organizations that claim to represent the interests of scholars. Heaven forfend that research cycles be distorted, when so many faculty do no research on any cycle whatsoever. The right of these professors to continue to do nothing, in the eyes of CAUT and OCUFA, must be protected against any serious appraisal. As the chair of English at San Jose State University wrote of his school's post-tenure review system, one of his part-time colleagues had said that she "had to earn her temporary job, year after year for seven years, with re-applications yearly, interviews, and subjection to critical scrutiny of her teaching and scholarship. She could not understand why we tenured professors should consider a review once every five years an imposition." Nor can we. Of course, there must be a process of third-party review before which an individual faculty member's non-renewal could be challenged.

Critics of renewable term appointments also suggest that the faculty's time will be spent in endless committee meetings studying the reappointment of their colleagues. This is possible; on the other hand, no one who has ever served on a present-day tenure committee at a university that takes tenure seriously could suggest that it does not consume endless hours and involve dozens of faculty auditing classes, reading books, and writing dozens of letters. We suspect that the cost in additional time would not be so great and, in any case, the time spent would be worthwhile it if it led to the sacking of those who do nothing other than discredit the very idea of a university as a place of scholarship. "Tenure is a privilege," wrote Jon Huer, a critic of the institution, "and all privileges eventually corrupt. Only periodic and pitiless self-criticism can retard the onset of routine corruption." This, it seems clear, is unlikely to emerge from within the Canadian academy.

Some will argue, of course, that if a single Canadian university — or all of them — did away with tenure, Canada would never get an academic star from abroad again. "The biggest argument for tenure is competition. We are competing with some of the largest universities in Canada and the United States for people," said the chair of a University of Alberta department. Frankly, this is twaddle. Margaret Thatcher's government effectively eliminated tenure in Britain, and while the universities suffered, it was more from budget cuts than the end of job security. There is almost no indication that academic freedom was jeopardized, even by the Iron Lady. Moreover, the academic heavyweights sought by the Alberta chair know they have no need for tenure; they have the best kind of job security, the kind that comes from accomplishment. It may be that junior scholars would have some concerns, but, here again, we believe this would not be so. The present job market is so overcrowded with able people who cannot find work that there would be dozens of applicants for every post; today, there are, sometimes, hundreds.

Others suggest cynically that if tenure is replaced by term contracts, hiring committees will deliberately select weak candidates for jobs. Then, when the competition gets fierce in a non-tenure university, the weak new appointees will be the first fired. Perhaps, but we don't think so. First, all of us have served on enough hiring committees to know that more often than not the best candidate does not necessarily get hired in a university system ruled by tenure. Too often, extraneous considerations enter: gender, race, age, the old-boy (and old-girl) net. Too often, weak departments replicate themselves, hiring those who will preserve the collegial attitudes of incompetence that make life at the University of Sloth so pleasant for all. As one colleague puts it, advertisements for jobs should read, "The qualified need not apply." Then, too, virtually every unionized university has a last-hired, first-fired clause that means that the junior faculty member, every one of whom has had to struggle to get onto the tenure track, is by definition the first to be let go in any financial crisis. The young might be demonstrably more able than the old, but the experienced grey beards would almost certainly survive the crunch. Worse yet, since so many women faculty have been recently hired, they will be disproportionately represented in any financial exigency firings.

We believe that term contracts are both right and proper and inevitable — and the best protection available for the young and able. They need not be axe-wielding sessions, with chortling (male) administrators washing the blood of martyred (women) professors off their hands. Like other financially strapped institutions, the University of Hawaii instituted limited-term contracts without bloodshed or fear. Responsibility was delegated downward to department chairs, peer-based standards were devised, and the review process was constructive.

"Faculty would not simply be written off as 'dead wood' or stigmatized as 'deficient,'" wrote Madeleine Goodman, but would have "an opportunity to improve their teaching skills or research capabilities with specially allocated resources for programs developed on a case-by-case basis." The University of Colorado and the California State University system also have included developmental aspects in their post-tenure review processes. In the first review cycle at Hawaii, 245 faculty were reviewed. Some 15 percent of these professors decided to retire, at least half influenced by the review process and presumably by frank conversations with their deans and chairs. This is a not-unusual result for those who can foresee the future and decide to leave; it is also generally a salutary outcome, since few of those who depart early in such circumstances would likely contribute much to the university's research profile. Of those who went through the process, 70 percent were in effect renewed and 22 percent were judged to have deficiencies in teaching, research, or service which had to be corrected. These faculty Goodman characterized into a typology — the mid-career slump, the aging faculty member, the alienated full professor, and the non-functioning professor. Every academic, every student, has met these types on every campus, where they poison the atmosphere and turn off students by the score.

At Hawaii, however, the administration and the professoriate set out to deal with the problems created by tenure and, to judge by Goodman's account, found a way to make the system work, though with much heartburn. Could Canadian universities not do the same? And if they did, would the public's perception of the universities not improve? To ask these questions is to answer them. Tenure has created the impression that professors do not work very hard for their (relatively) high salaries, with their six- to 8-hour teaching loads each week and four-month summer breaks. We know that this is untrue for many of our colleagues, but it is a damningly correct judgment on far too many in the system. There is no justification now, if there ever was, for this "profscam," and the all-but-unassailable job security afforded by tenure is the main roadblock to fixing matters. Even some supporters of tenure as a shield for academic freedom have come to the conclusion that tenure has been abused. Economist John Crispo believes that tenure should only "prevail as long as one is performing effectively in an appropriate combination of research, scholarship, teaching and related activities. If faculty members are not carrying out their responsibilities, tenure should not protect them." If CAUT, faculty associations, and university administrators treated tenure as it was intended, and if they actually rooted out the incompetent, there would be no difficulty. But they will not act.

The only answer, therefore, is limited-term, renewable contracts. The good faculty — the competent researchers and the effective teachers — will have no trouble continuing their careers successfully under this regime. With luck and some administrative courage, the deadwood, no longer protected by job-security tenure, will be pruned at last.

Chapter 7

Publish and Perish:
Rituals, Print, and the Universities

UNTIL RECENTLY, students arriving at Canadian universities in the fall could be certain of one thing: every year, every month, every day, there were more books in the library, more journals on the shelf, more information. And increasingly as the century wore on and we approached the millennium, there were new varieties of information: online services, Internet sites, and computers galore. More, it would seem, of everything — and more, of course, is better. Or is it?

Many of the books are unread, the journals unthumbed, the computers clogged with Internet advertising, the work stations jammed with student e-mailers. Desperate librarians whittle away at their staff to meet shrinking budgetary targets and then, alternatives exhausted, start hacking at journal and book budgets.

Money, or the lack of it, is to blame for some of the unhappiness in today's libraries. Crowded stacks, overloaded computer terminals, and overburdened staff can be attributed to lack of budgets. At some universities, professors are told not to add new books to their course lists because the university cannot afford to buy them. These are serious problems. Some forms of knowledge are quickly dated. New discoveries and unexpected insights from the millions of academics around the world must be accommodated.

So the argument goes, and much of it is true. Many library budgets are simply too low. New books do contain new knowledge, and journal articles are essential to keeping up both with the latest scholarship and the competition from other universities. Take the sad case of the University of New Brunswick. To assist the teaching of Twentieth-Century American History plus International Relations since 1648, there was in 1996 a library budget of $1767.64. Standard periodicals ate up $1580 of that sum, leaving $187.64 for books in fields where annual publications number not in the hundreds but the thousands. The average cost of a scholarly book in these areas is about $50, which translates into three and a half books per annum.

What does it mean? Administrators may nod sagely and murmur that history professors are slaves to the text. After all, history is history; it all happened, didn't it? And don't forget the Internet, with its reams and reams of pictures, home pages, and other information. There is no disputing that these answers are unrealistic and insufficient, since even in the late 1990s most information and analysis in history and other fields are still published in print form. Perhaps students at UNB will not need to be right up to date, or even remotely up to date. And since UNB is not unique in starving its library budgets, there will be plenty of other Canadian students in the same boat. There might be consequences in the short term — students emigrating to other countries, professors refusing to come — but students can always be replaced with a dip in admission standards, and there are plenty of starving PhDs who would accept the inconvenience of a dearth of books.

The result is not all bad. There is an unstated assumption in the argument we have just presented that books and journals, and their electronic cousins, are all about conveying information. But this idea is not entirely true. Books and articles are also a measuring device. "My library is bigger than your library," universities tell one another. "More books mean more knowledge and therefore more opportunity. Come to my university." This argument also has its merits, including a fair proportion of truth.

Knowledge isn't all that books measure. "My professor writes more books and articles than your professor — though not as many as Pierre Berton or Peter Newman, of course," the argument continues. "Better still, lots of my professors, taken in the aggregate, write more than your professors. Come to my university or, better yet, give it money." And, up to a point, that is also a rational conclusion.

Book writing is a sign of life. If nothing else, you know that something is going on at a university when you see that its professors have produced, on the average, three books per head. You could deduce that this activity was encouraged at the university, and you would probably be right. You might even guess that book writers receive not only approbation but some form of monetary reward. Right again — in some places. Books mean more points on the salary scale, more merit, and more pay — at least in those places that measure performance, as opposed to longevity, and reward it.

And, within limits, there is nothing wrong with this approach. Taken in moderation, books and articles show that a professor does something professional outside the classroom. Carried to logical extremes, however, the evaluation system becomes "publish or perish."

Why do we say "measure" or "count" when we refer to our colleagues' publications? Why not say "read"? The answer is that, with a few exceptions, publications and people, academics do not read one another's work. This is partly because of professionalization and specialization, but also because of quantity. There are now so many journals, books, and articles that all but a few cataloguers will not know and cannot know how many journals are published in a field such as "physics" or "history." Even if we narrow the field to, say, "American history," the task is daunting. We admit that it might still be possible in a given year to read everything written on the history of the Maritime provinces, for example, but it would be a chore that only the professionally interested will take the time to perform.

And that is to consider quantity alone. With quantity we are on fairly safe ground. But what of quality? That is less certain. There are values to consider, and somebody's values are somebody else's vices. Values command less than universal agreement. Before we consider the vexed question of quality, let us turn back to quantity, to counting. We mentioned above the positive incentives offered for publishing. There are negative incentives, too. There is, above all, the imperative to publish.

Publish what? Forms of publication vary. Some disciplines, especially the sciences and the social sciences, prefer "journal" articles — in magazines run by and for the professionals who contribute and subscribe. There is a pecking order in journals which can be quite strict. In economics, for example, an article in *The Journal of Political Economy*, from the University of Chicago, is at the top. An article in its Canadian counterpart, the *Canadian Journal of Economics*, is not at the same level; it is, indeed, whispered to be a refuge for graduate students peddling their conference papers.

Economists as a general rule do not write books. That has not always been the case. John Maynard Keynes wrote his *General Theory of Employment, Interest and Money* in book form. John Kenneth Galbraith, the Canadian-born Harvard economist, has a long and varied book curriculum, including memoirs and diary; but then, Galbraith has had a vastly more interesting life than most academics. When a University of Toronto economist, David Foot, published *Boom, Bust & Echo*, an actual best-seller on his subject, demographics, in 1996, it was a banner event. No one could remember when this had last happened to an economist[1], and academic economists of the more mathematical school were not at all sure what to make of this feat.

In political science, the situation is similar. There are journals, and then there are journals. Political scientists do write books, and some have sold fairly well, though to do that they need a market outside Canada. Perhaps the best-seller in Canada, apart from textbook authors, was Jack Macleod, another University of Toronto professor, who wrote two novels satirizing academic life.

We could go down the list, from English to history to physics: there are plenty of publications, and there is obviously much research. The results are appraised rather like the medal standings at the Olympics, and academic administrators have worked out elaborate formulas to measure individual and collective merit. These calculations

---

1. Unlike Canada's last economist icon, Harold Innis, Foot is actually readable.

are designed to show that the staff at one university has the edge over the professors at another. They have more publications, and more references in other people's footnotes. The beat goes on, every year at a more frantic pace.

"The emphasis on number of publications as a prerequisite for advancement is so great that many people use the salami method — slicing every paper into six or seven papers prior to publication." Theses are regularly butchered into a number of articles, and then the parts are sewn back together for the first, job-winning book. What used to be an exercise in originality or brain power has degenerated into a preoccupation with dollars.

There are several forms of justification for dollar dispensation. Most important, there is the reward for professionalism, which dictates that inhabitants of a particular discipline demonstrate their mastery of the craft. This is accomplished through passing exams, but in an age where university graduates in Canada number in the millions, and where even PhDs increase at the rate of 3300 per annum (1993 figures), the examination requirement has become inflated. In the 1890s, a Bachelor of Arts degree, in English Canada preferably from Oxford, was enough; by the 1920s a Master of Arts was generally expected; and by the 1940s a full Doctor of Philosophy was imposed as necessary for permanent employment. Beginning professors seeking "tenure stream" appointments did not need to have their doctorate in hand until the 1970s, but by the end of that decade supply had so far outstripped demand that it became necessary to insist on a new criterion: a book.

Recently, at a large Canadian university, a hiring committee found itself confronting no fewer than forty-one applications (in some fields, like Canadian history, there could be as many as 150 applicants), all from PhDs. After winnowing and narrowing by field, it arrived at eight — all Canadians (our immigration laws demand no less), and all with books plus articles. Some had two books and some, indeed, had more publications than those on the committee hiring them. Not long ago, a book was generally considered cause for tenure and promotion to associate professor, the lowest permanent rank. Two books would boost you up to full professor, after which, the summit attained, you could rest on your laurels. This leisurely progress is still true at the upper exalted ranks of professordom, because most full professors were promoted long ago, under the easier rules, but it is not true lower down. It is one of the issues that divides juniors from seniors, the old from the young, gerontocracy from youth.

Rewards are positive or negative. Positive means more hiring, more pay, and progress through the ranks. "College presidents do a lot of talking about the need for faculty to do more teaching and less publishing, but when it comes to tenure, if you haven't published, bang, you're out," according to the editor of a journal called *Magazines for Libraries*. "Modern academics are pretty much chosen to be virtual 'publication machines,' whether or not they actually have something compelling to publish," writes a Toronto psychologist.[2] This is an exaggeration as far as existing faculty members are concerned, but it is deadly accurate for those seeking to get their first post.

Youth publishes because it wants to, perhaps, but also because it must. Is this an improvement? It certainly belies the image of the lazy professor, stimulating instead a vision of frantic and desperate activity. But in what context should we view the product, and to what end is all this energy directed?

Publication derives from professionalization, clearly enough. Qualification for professional status gives publication its first boost. Yet greater standards — we are not sure about "higher" standards — have not prevented the proliferation of professors. As the bar is raised, the jumps get higher, and still the professors come on. As professors multiply, they specialize. This is also one of the characteristics of professionalization.

Professors at the turn of the century were jacks of all trades. Knowledge as presented in books was relatively limited, so it was possible

---

2. Robert Woods, "Modern Academics Forced to Be Publication Machines," letter to *Toronto Star*, 19 August 1996.

to have greater breadth. In universities, this breadth was translated into professors who swotted up their lectures from texts just a few hours ahead of their students. The result wasn't very deep, but it certainly was comprehensive: it challenged professors' energy and consumed their time.

This pattern has not completely disappeared. At community colleges, and in certain institutions like Toronto's Ryerson Polytechnic University, "service professors" — the term is ours — still teach a range of courses and a lot of them. It is an older pattern of learning, but for undergraduates not necessarily an inferior one.

The lush government handouts of the 1960s — gratefully received by special-interest groups — encouraged professionals, including professors, to do what they do best — multiply and specialize. Figures for medicare, for legal aid, and for university grants tell the story.

More professors meant more articles and more books, and consequently more journals and more publishers. A professional subgroup like Canadian history was once serviced, in English, by one journal. By the early 1970s there were four or five Canadian history journals, plus a few dedicated to servicing Canadian historians of non-Canadian subjects. Now there are over twenty history journals in Canada. There is the venerable *Canadian Historical Review*, which currently caters in its articles and reviews primarily to social and leftist history. There is *Labour/Le Travail*, which does the same thing, and *Social History*, which does what its title promises, and *Socialist Studies*, whose objective is carried on its masthead. There is the *Canadian Journal of History*, which covers non-Canadian subjects, not to mention *Acadiensis*, *Ontario History*, *BC Studies*, the *Revue d'Histoire de l'Amérique française*, *Mediaeval Studies*, the *Journal of Canadian Art History*, the *Canadian Bulletin of Medical History*, *Archivaria*, the *International Journal of Maritime History*, and *Theatre Research in Canada/Histoire du Théâtre au Canada*. The maximum circulation of any of these reviews is about 2000; most are a good deal less.

History is not alone in print proliferation. There is *Ariel: A Review of International English Literature*, the *Journal of Distance Education/*

Revue de l'enseignement à distance, the *Canadian Journal of Film Studies*, *Recherches féministes*, the *Osgoode Hall Law Journal*, *Atlantis*, the *Canadian Journal of Linguistics*, the *Canadian Journal of Criminology*, *International Journal*, and *Etudes internationales*. All these and many more (141 in all, in 1994–95) are subsidized by the federal government, through the Social Sciences and Humanities Research Council. There are other sources and other journals for the harder sciences, and, of course, the federal government is not the only player in the journal funding game.

How could this be? The important thing to bear in mind is that these journals exist primarily for their writers and contributors, not for their readers. The groundwork for the proliferation of journals was laid by specialization, supported by rising government grants to universities, so there were more historians, more film studiers, more international specialists, more law professors than ever before. This specialization ended in most places the old jack-of-all-trades profession and created a new and much more personally oriented one. Historians — or political scientists, economists, and so on — were no longer obliged to spend their time spreading their wisdom over unfamiliar fields. Instead, they could cultivate their own gardens, right here, right now. And only "their" gardens. No irrigation for the neighbour: there was no need to share when there was money enough for all. And if there was not, the government could print or borrow some more. The government obliged.

This situation was not confined to Canada. To some degree it reproduced itself all over the Western world. Canada was part of an international academic market and, for a few brief years around 1970, it was a sellers' market. Small wonder that the sellers took advantage of an unprecedented opportunity to remake their professional lives.

And so the ritual of publication — one article, two articles, one book, two books, THREE books — became more and more specialized. And there were more journals to publish in, and more publishers to cater to demands that a few years earlier would have been thought preposterous. And why not? In the budgetary climate of the 1970s, you had merely to step up to the table to be served. If there were a few more journals, so what?

Better still, there were new mechanisms in place to safeguard the sanctity of the publication rite. Journals were not only prized as journals but as *refereed* journals. No longer would a journal bear the imprint of a single editor; instead, there were editorial boards on the masthead, carefully chosen to reflect diversity of origin and interest. "Come let us reason together" became the subliminal motto. Decisions were exported from editors to outside readers. Using outside appraisers was not unknown before, if an editor felt uncertain, but now it became *de rigueur*. And there was the "double-blind" system, in which the reviewer was not told the name of the author, nor the author that of the reviewer.[3] The result was probably much the same as with a single editor or an editorial team, but it was in tune with the cautious and suspicious spirit of the age.

Refereed journals made for a first-class "count." According to a staffer at the Institute for Scientific Information, which counts the number of times an article is cited in other refereed publications, "the requests we receive to check citation frequency have doubled from year to year." It's a wonderful way to compute the velocity of ideas, especially in a time of budget cuts. Is a journal *really* significant and useful? Is a professor *really* worth her salt and salary? Continued the staffer: "The people who pay the bills for these publications are coming under increasing financial stress, and they come to us for an independent opinion about what is useful and what is not."

Now let us return to the theme with which we began this chapter. More journals + more articles = more knowledge, but also more disunity, disguised as individualism. There was then and there is now a lot

---

3. It must not be thought that journals or academics were the only practitioners of the system of responsibility avoidance. Corporate boards of directors hired consultants — impartial — to tell them what to do, executive search committees hired head-hunters, and so on. The process of decision making in late twentieth-century society has become a lengthy and costly business. On the other hand, paranoids may have been appeased.

more to read. That in itself makes the maintenance of a unified profession difficult, but what did that matter in the 1960s and 1970s? The 1970s were not a decade of difficult choices, or any choice at all, save one. If you disagreed, you could always found your own journal. The money could always be unearthed to fund this or that new publication. The lowest common denominator, the path of least resistance — that was the obvious choice. The age of subsidy had arrived.

The process was also driven by the overpowering and universally admitted need to get published. The rituals of professionalization required it, specialization made it less of an intellectual strain, and grants for research and grants for publication made it possible. The language used to justify these phenomena suffered a round of inflation, but in an inflationary era, who noticed?

What were the results? They were not universally bad. As promised, we have it in our power to learn about an amazing number of facts and theories. Analyses that might have had difficulty seeing the light of day a few years before were published more easily and more rapidly than they would have been. It is hard to say whether intellectual fashions changed more rapidly as a result, but that is possible.

As Noel Malcolm, a historian, wrote in the British newspaper *The Independent* in the summer of 1996: "Where real research is concerned, [publication] is no bad thing, especially in the natural sciences where it leads to a genuine accumulation of knowledge. But," he adds, and it's an important *but*, "most of the books published today, in the humanities at least, are not presentations of hitherto unknown facts. They are unoriginal interpretative rehashes of what is already known." It is, he says later, all "unnecessary work."[4]

Some professors used the opportunity afforded by plentiful, subsidized journals to publish nonsense, but that had always been so. In a permissive and lucrative age, however, there was less likely to be mortal combat over ideas, and if there was, it was more likely to occur in

---

4. Noel Malcolm, "Sinking in a Sea of Words," *The Independent on Sunday*, 21 July 1996.

the letters column of the *Globe and Mail* than in the pages of scholarly books and learned journals that nobody read.

That was the key: everyone bought and nobody read. And "everyone" was such a large number it was hard to take seriously; as for "nobody," that wasn't the point. What mattered was the citation in the Curriculum Vitae, the count, and the promotion and salary raise. If nobody read, why worry? In the Age of Plenty, the Age of Nonsense could flourish, too.

Do we exaggerate? We think not. A study of academic publication recently concluded that "of all the articles published in even the most prestigious natural and social science journals, less than one-half were ever cited by anyone." Some citations proved to be authors quoting themselves, but what did it matter as long as they fell into the Great Count? The Carnegie Foundation for the Advancement of Teaching found that half of a sample among the professoriate were persuaded that "their publications were merely counted, never read, even by those in the personnel process who insist on those same publications as a prerequisite for tenure or promotion."[5]

The proposition that much of today's research effort is, by any reasonable standards, meaningless has received some attention in the United States and Great Britain, but little in Canada. "I am not exaggerating," Malcolm continued in his article in *The Independent*, "when I say that this flood [of publications] is eroding academic intellectual life." Harking back to the late 1970s — when the flood was already overflowing the banks — he recalls that he was able to read more or less everything in his "field" of knowledge, seventeenth-century philosophy. That, he observes, is no longer possible in the late 1990s. Not only can he not read everything, "nor would [he] want to." The main cost of the multiplication of publications, according to Malcolm, is the subversion of knowledge, or what used to be called "the Republic of Letters," the

---

5. Carnegie study cited in William T. Daly, "Teaching and Scholarship: Adapting American Higher Education to Hard Times," *Journal of Higher Education* 65, 1 (1994): 47.

common ground of culture. We are inclined to agree, but let us not forget that pointless research has other costs, computed both in grants and in lost faculty time.

Some have drawn the conclusion that faculty might possibly be encouraged to do something else. At Stanford University in California, where research has been much prized over time, the president recently suggested an upper limit on the *number* of publications any faculty member could submit for consideration by personnel bodies.

Certainly there is too much to read, and the profusion also helped to undermine the common identity of the academic profession. With no single focus but, instead, a thousand points of light, each sparkling with subsidy, it was natural to lose sight of any common interest. Disciplines have fragmented into academic boutiques whose proprietors are reluctant to admit any form of common interest, except perhaps in the face of an external threat.

The result was not a land of intellectual plenty but an academic desert. The flavour of modern academic discourse was caught by a *New York Times* reporter in 1994. Time was, he wrote, when "the arrival of the latest issue of a scholarly journal devoted to the arts and humanities or the social sciences would send professors scurrying into their hideaways to devour a broadly illuminating article by John Maynard Keynes, John Dewey or perhaps William James." But not today. "There isn't the same attention paid to them now that there used to be," John Kenneth Galbraith told the *Times*. "I must say my own reading of them has become highly selective." Galbraith is, after all, pushing ninety, and has more than earned the right to check out. Yet he is certainly not alone, and not even in the minority.

Libraries, oppressed by the cost of subscriptions, have long cast an anxious eye on their books and journals. There are two contradictory trends as far as libraries are concerned. The number of books published annually, the world around, has risen from 521,000 in 1970 to 863,000 in 1991 (UNESCO figures). But library budgets have shrunk in the same period. On a per-student basis, the budgets of Canadian university libraries sank by 22 percent between 1980 and 1993 — using constant dollars. At the same time, enterprising publishers hiked the subscription costs for journals, with admirable results for their balance sheets (one well-known journal publisher in England turned an after-tax profit of $225 million in 1994) and correspondingly depressing effects on university libraries.

"A minority of titles accounts for a majority of uses," one study of library use concludes, and "books and journals are subject to rapid rates of aging and obsolescence." In a sampling of the use of science journals, the percentage of journal titles used ranged from 37 percent to less than 10 percent. In fact, in three of six libraries studied, the rate of usage was right at the lower end.[6] We can also learn from the experience of the Louisiana State University library, which in 1993 cancelled subscriptions to 1569 journals. The library told its clients, faculty and students, that the library would procure copies of any article requested from the cancelled journals and provide it free. In the two years following, the library filled 2092 requests of this kind, an average of just over seven per journal. The cost of the articles to the university was US$25,000; the saving from cancelled journals, US$900,000. Even in science, the citadel of scholarly publishing, the balance against current journal practice seems clear.[7]

Although we think academics are reading as many books as they ever did, they do not, and often cannot, read as broadly as they once did. And reading some books may be worse than reading none at all. Let us turn briefly to the way academics write. What has increased professionalism brought to the art of communication? Or, more bluntly, why would anybody want to read what academics write?

---

6. Dennis P. Carrigan, "Commercial Journal Publishers and University Libraries: Retrospect and Prospect," *Journal of Scholarly Publishing* 27, 4 (1996): 211–212.

7. Readers might wish to know what the costs of journals can be. The highest prices are in science, a field diligently mined by acquisitive private-sector publishers for many years. *Neuroscience*, for example, cost US$3775 a year in 1995; *Nuclear Physics B* cost US$10,775; *Brain Research* cost US$14,000.

Academics, as a group, do not write very well. That fact was brought home to an unwitting and, after a point, unwilling consumer of their product. Bronwyn Drainie, a Toronto broadcaster and writer, was made a judge for a major Canadian book prize. Her mandate was to review Canadian non-fiction and, as she discovered, there was quite a bit of it. She was surprised by what she found, and she did not like it.

Like many book-buyers and book-lovers, Drainie was unfamiliar with the output of Canada's university presses. There are a fair number of these publishers, and they produce a lot of books — more than 300 each year. Most Canadians, even most Canadian book-buyers, do not know them or their product. That is not surprising, though not entirely justified.[8]

Most bookstores outside those on university campuses typically do not stock university press books, nor do public libraries buy many of their products.[9] Occasionally one or two fight their way through, but that is an uphill struggle. Bookstores do not see why they should confide scarce shelf space to most university press books, which do not sell, nor do public libraries see why they should buy copies of books that few if any of their subscribers will want to borrow, let alone read.

This is a prejudice, and university press books (and their authors) suffer the consequences. As prejudices go, however, this one has something to be said for it.

Let us consider Drainie's experience as a book-prize judge. Her task, she discovered, included reviewing titles like *Invisible Leviathan: The Marxist Critique of Market Despotism beyond Postmodernism* or *Hope and Deception in Conception Bay: Merchant-Settler Relations in Newfoundland, 1785–1855*. These titles, we assure the reader, are not the most bizarre in the catalogue. She might have cited *Sculptors and Physicians in Fifth-Century Greece: A Preliminary Study* (presumably with another

8. Some university press products are extremely handsome specimens of the printer's art: *The Historical Atlas of Canada* in three volumes is one such example.

9. All three of us, as frequent university press authors, can testify to this ignorance, and we certainly do not think it justified!

version to follow), or *Rereading Middle English Romance*, or *Pierrot in Petrograd*, subtitled *Commedia dell'Arte/Balagan in Twentieth-Century Russian Theatre and Drama*.

The least that can be said about these books is that they are specialized. They are also all subsidized. Subsidy does not always mean that a book is bad any more than clumsy titles always indicate that an arid reading experience lies within your grasp. Subsidy may only mean that a publisher has a fairly well-founded belief that a book will not sell, and the more specialized the topic, the smaller the likely audience. And, of course, the publisher does not wish to take the risk that even a gripping title like *Zambian Crisis Behaviour* will not convert browsers into buyers.

But can one usually judge a book by its cover? Usually, yes. Drainie found the contents of these books, and others, mystifying. Why were they published? she asked. "Making decisions based on quality is part of what publishing is supposed to be about, isn't it?" It was a naive question. Academic publishers, like commercial publishers, do reject books, and it is true to say that the manuscripts or would-be books that they return to senders are worse, on the average, than the ones they publish. The ones they do publish, however, are often things that only an academic could love.

University presses publish plenty of titles, but in considering plenty we should also consider the context. Canadian publishers — including university presses — published 5900 titles in 1990–91, of which 1226 were "texts," 3342 "trade" (aimed at the general reader), and 1292 "other," which might include some of the obscure titles we have referred to. That year, net sales in English earned $996 million for publishing companies. The trend since then has been either down or flat. In 1993–94, before consumer spending had climbed out of the trough of recession, Canadian publishers made $980 million, for 6725 titles.

These are not large figures, certainly not in relation to gross national product or to leisure spending generally. And, of course, English Canada by itself has only twenty-three million people, of whom many use English as a second language. Ninety percent of Canadians admit to perusing a newspaper within a twelve-month period, 80 percent a magazine, and 66 percent a book. Women (75 percent) are more likely to read a book than men (59 percent).

As the head of Canada's academic book subsidy program admits, print runs for academic books are low and are sinking fast. In the 1970s it was not uncommon to publish 1000–1200 copies of an academic book. Most of that run could reliably be sold to libraries, within a year or two. In the 1980s, 700 copies were a more common total, and in the 1990s, 400. Even at this figure, unsold copies linger in the publisher's inventory — sometimes more than half. In one case, a publisher reported sales of two, presumably leaving 500 on the shelf, unwanted, unread, and unsold.[10]

A publishing run of 400 or 600 copies is not commercially viable. An academic book costs about $40,000 to produce, including editing, paper, printing, binding, distribution, plus other overhead. Price is usually high — in 1997 usually in the range of $60 for a medium-size hard-cover book. *Invisible Leviathan*, which Drainie found so unpalatable, would have cost her $49.50 had she found it in a bookstore.

But *Invisible Leviathan* had an advantage that guaranteed that it would be published. It was subsidized. There are subsidies and then there are…subsidies. Company histories, legal biographies, local chronicles, even autobiographies of prominent politicians are often made attractive to publishers with the promise of money, up-front and guaranteed. And there are few publishers, commercial or academic, too proud to refuse the inducement.

For academic books, however, there is a regular process. Aspiring authors submit their treasured manuscript to a publisher, the publisher has it read and appraised by peer review, and sends it on to a federally funded program, the Aid to Scholarly Publications Program in Ottawa

---

10. "I hope it was a mistake," Michael J. Carley added. He meant a mistake in reporting, but he might just as well mean a mistake in publishing in the first place, not to say a mistake in subsidizing. M.J. Carley, "The State of Scholarly Publishing in Canada," a June 1995 address, to be found on the ASPP website, Social Sciences and Humanities Federation of Canada.

(ASPP for short). The ASPP then has the manuscript peer reviewed and, depending on the reports, and whether the author has bowed sufficiently to the current scholarly gods of "say no evil," it gives money. A common grant is $8,000, and in 1994–95 such grants totalled $1,034,000. Publication then follows.

Evidence as to who publishes what is anecdotal. "English PhDs as far as I'm concerned are absolutely the worst," one publisher claimed. "Historians at least read one another's works, and buy them. English professors don't read each other, and buy only novels."

What gets subsidized? Well, *Pierrot in Petrograd* got subsidized. *A.J.M. Smith, Canadian Metaphysical*, got published, as did *Creating States: Studies in the Performinative Language of John Milton and William Blake* and *Territorial Disputes: Maps and Mapping Strategies in Contemporary Canadian and Australian Fiction*. Racy titles these, obviously designed to leap off the shelf and grab the pocketbook of a prospective purchaser. But no bookstore in its right mind would order these books: the shelf they are destined for is a library shelf, for consultation, perhaps, by specialized scholars.

Does this matter? These are "academic" titles. Whoever said academics had to show imagination, particularly in the use or abuse of language? Shouldn't academic books properly remain the concern of academics? Doesn't Drainie's reaction demonstrate the gulf between an unspecialized public and a highly specialized industry? Why should we expect anything different from university presses, and anyway, would different be better?

Yes, it matters, and no, academic books should not be the concern solely of academics. And, most important, different would be better. We won't ask, How could things be worse? They could be. But what exists should be improved, drastically.

Surely we, the authors, have fallen into the sin of judging a book by its cover — or worse, by its title. What about content? What about form? Once found and opened, in a library rather than a bookstore, academic writing presents some challenges. Again, we should not exaggerate. There is good writing from academics and there is bad. Some books from university presses make a pleasurable read, and some do not. It is even possible to sketch out a reading list of university press books, published in Canada, that can be read for fun.

It is also possible to list books that read as if they had been written by sausages. Sausage-authors are particularly attracted to words like "hegemon" and its derivatives and they enjoy examining questions from what they term a "realist" or "critical theory perspective." We tend to think the worst writing comes from English faculties, or from political scientists, but then we are historians and subject to professional deformation and prejudice. To be fair, let us simply admit that the standard of writing across academia, including history, is low.

What is true of books is even more true of journals. There are currently about 18,000 journals worldwide. The United States, with the largest number of professors and the richest university system, dominates the field. The result has been the proliferation of an international journal style, so that reading journals, subject matter apart, is a homogenizing experience.

Journals, as much as university press books, speak to their own professional enclaves. They do nothing to lessen the gap between the humanities and the social sciences, or between the arts and the sciences. Sometimes, indeed, editors gaze wistfully across the intellectual gulfs and seek to transplant blooms from one field into another; but the result, usually, is more incomprehension.

There was a spectacular example of the lack of common understanding in 1996. Many academics find journals just as dull as the general public would, and they often treat them as subjects of satire. The temptation to play jokes on serious-minded editors and their sober following is sometimes irresistible, as happened in the cultural studies journal *Social Text*, an American publication. A mathematical physicist, Adam Sokal, decided to test *Social Text*'s reflexes. Its editors, he believed, were so committed to their own brand of cultural nihilism — of the postmodernist variety — that they would swallow any nonsense that seemed to support their point. He cobbled together a number of false propositions, tricked them out in the appropriate postmodernist jargon, asserted that they "proved" that science could not be objective (one of the main tenets of postmodernism), and awaited the result.

Sokal was overjoyed when his article was accepted — promptly accepted — and published. Then he revealed his hoax, to the rage and dismay of the editors of *Social Text* and their following. Though one of the principles of postmodernism is that things are not what they seem, the editors had taken Sokal at face value, perhaps believing that a mathematical physicist was incapable of deception. But he was, and he had demonstrated that any nonsense, seriously presented and clothed in the proper jargon, will do the trick at least in some journals.

Scientists may take some pride over the incident: after all, the ignorance and prejudice of social scientists — "soft" scientists — was revealed once more. But hard scientists have their problems too. In August 1996 the Natural Sciences and Engineering Research Council, the principal granting agency for science in Canada, sent its clientele some unpleasant news. They would, in future, have to explain their projects in layman's language, plain English or plain French, this being a bilingual agency. The reason was that the politicians who pay the money that is converted into grants were questioning the research they were funding, and the NSERC staff had to confess that they themselves were at sea as to what, exactly, they were funding.

Opaque prose does not lead to clarity of thought or clarity of meaning. The proposition should be self-evident, and it is — anywhere except in universities and, of course, in the kingdom of the learned journals.

Take a recent example, far from the worst, a prize-winning article in the *International Journal*. The *International Journal* used to be published for Canadians who were interested in foreign affairs. Over time it was converted into a political science journal aimed at "professionals" — that is, other political scientists. Every year it awards a prize to the most promising article by a young scholar, and in 1996 the award winner was entitled, "If You Want to Prosper, Accept Decline: The Absolute Gains Problem for Competition."

Those who have the stamina to plough through the article will discover that the author wishes to examine theories that explain why, in

certain circumstances, powerful states will do better to accept temporary setbacks in hopes of a better future. It is a learned discussion and
in most respects a sensible one. But there is a flaw: the author writes
according to the standards of his chosen profession. Clarity is sacrificed
for a phantom precision, expressed in a kind of Stalinoid jargon. "As
the neorealist-neoliberal debate progressed," the author helpfully
explains at one point, "observers began to fault its ratiocination."
Hegemons, neorealists, and neoliberals lumber around the article, the
terms conveying about as much meaning as "Montanists" and "Mono-
physites" — forgotten sectarians from early Christian history whose
theories once had the drawing power for the gullible that deconstruc-
tion and semiotics have for the gullible today.

But we digress. This is an article that demands concentration, even
though the temptation to wander — to the fridge, to the television —
is well nigh irresistible while trying to read it. Take this sentence, which
deals with states' occasional reluctance to resort to war: "Institutions
can moderate the demands of a self-help system, and military violence
is no longer the fungible instrument it once was." *Fungible*, in case
the reader has not encountered it before, is defined as "being of such
a nature or kind as to be freely exchangeable or replaceable." We are
not sure that knowing the definition really clarifies the meaning of
the sentence.

We did not select this piece of prose because it is notably bad, but
because in terms of its author's professional expectations it is good. It is
not completely unintelligible: its main shortcoming is its clotted prose,
obscuring meaning while conveying great and nearly exclusive learning. We could have chosen worse, because the academic fads of the
1990s as embodied in books and articles offer a rich field for ridicule.

Let us not exaggerate. The usual prose in academic journals or
academic books is dull normal. Horrors there are, but they are not the
rule. The general impression is not one of error, but of trivia and trivia's
first cousin, tedium. It is trivial because the form, not the content, of
learning is what counts. The 18,000 journals, the tens of thousands of
books published each year, exist because, up until now, the money has

always been there to buy the journals for libraries, to pay the editorial staffs, to sustain the research that wends its way into article or book form.

There are sporadic attempts to remedy the situation. Granting agencies from time to time toy with the idea of cutting off subsidies to the least-read journals — those with a circulation, say, of less than 400. A normal observer might think that was the least a granter could do in a time of budget cuts: better save what can be saved rather than risk it all. But no. At the hint of such a heretical suggestion the doors of the academic castle swing open and the trumpet sounds for the special interests to assemble and march to battle. Such a battle was fought at the Social Sciences and Humanities Research Council in the fall of 1996, and it was lost. The beat, or rather the count, goes on.

The cumulative count of academic publishing has served only one interest — that of the people doing the publishing. It has ignored readers, and it has paid the price. University press publishing in particular, academic publishing in general, is discredited even among academics. Few books pass the ultimate test of purchase even among those who produce them and in other ways support the academic publishing-counting system.

Fewer books would be better books. Books written to be read and bought would have to meet a standard of literacy that would be notably higher than academic books presently meet. Indeed, it is arguable that the standard of prose in Harlequin Romances is higher than the norm among academic authors. Fewer books but longer print runs would mean books that cost less. And fewer books might even mean more copies sold, not less.

It was a luxury to create and sustain a scholarly publication ritual even in the 1960s, when the living was easy. In the 1990s the system is creaking at the seams. And just when the money is running out.

———

Money was the magic elixir of the 1970s, the solution to whatever ailed man, woman, or beast. Now the money has run out, something that academics deplore — in company with every other interest group in our society, even businessmen. But let us turn the question around. Can it be that lack of money will be the solution to the problems of the late 1990s?

At first blush, the cost of subsidizing academic books and journals in Canada is not large. Books alone cost $1 million in overt subsidies in 1994–5. We should bear in mind that subsidy is a small part of the ultimate problem: the purchase of books and journals for libraries. English Canada is, after all, only around 5 percent of the English-speaking world, and most books and journals come from the United States or the United Kingdom.

We would not deny that subsidies have had some beneficial effect. If we apply the law of averages, half the subsidy decisions are probably justified in terms of the subsidy-granting agencies; and we have no special reason to think that many of those decisions over time are wrong. The same effect might be achieved by positioning the manuscripts at the top of a very long staircase and pushing, but we recognize that staircases do not have quite the same ritual cachet as peer selection and the careful deliberation of juries.

Again, the authors of this book have generally been treated very well by the ASPP or other funding agencies. The system, however, is peculiar. We believe there is sometimes bias against individual authors or points of view. It is also true that some university presses have become inordinately devoted to the subsidy game, to the point where the removal of the established subsidy engine might force them to shut down entirely.[11] This matters because, in a very tight academic job market, to have published a book is critical in getting a young scholar a job. There are delays of up to eighteen months as authors are made to make changes to satisfy the demands of sometimes foolish, sometimes

11. Association of Universities and Colleges of Canada–Canadian Association of Research Libraries [AUCC–CARL], "The Changing World of Scholarly Communication: Challenges and Choices for Canada," November 1996, AUCC Website.

ideologically deterministic, ASPP readers who, moreover, ordinarily take months to reply. They are not paid, and the ASPP often gets what it pays for. Sometimes, if there is divided counsel in the assessments, additional appraisals are demanded. Equally unfortunate, the whole system does little for standards and nothing for publishing. The books are almost always unreadable by all but the few experts in the particular field, for one thing. And university presses in Canada are unable to make publishing decisions on their own, so chained are they to the ASPP. In our view, it would be better to eliminate the ASPP, to give the university presses a block grant, and to let them decide through their own processes what books to publish.[12]

Yes, scholarly appraisals must remain. Yes, there must be some overview of how the money is employed. But this simple proposal would eliminate a costly bureaucracy in the ASPP and put the responsibility where it belongs: on academics to write good books and on university presses to publish them. The middleman (middleperson?) is unnecessary, counter-productive, and much too open to biased behaviour. A system created from the best of motives and designed to raise standards has failed, become corrupt in the eyes of many, and should be eliminated.

The real harm lies not in the cosy games of grantsmanship. Subsidies simply produce too many books that no one ever reads, and these too many books degrade the market for, and reputation of, those books that might once have found an audience.

As we have suggested, the problem does not lie in the way standards are applied but in the principal reason why the standards are necessary. That reason is ritual professionalism, the professionalism that has turned academic professionals into "publication machines." The problems are not new. As we have defined them so far, they include:

---

12. We have a caveat. Distributing block grants on the basis of current publication ratios would have the effect of freezing publishers in place, relative to one another. A strict prorating of grants would therefore prove counterproductive in the longer run, as disproportion becomes inequity.

- ritual professionalism, characterized by the demand that the professoriate publish, and publish on paper between covers;
- avoidance of decision making, characterized in academia (as elsewhere) by the mania for counting;
- excessive specialization, characterized by boutique learning; and
- a weakness for jargon, characterized by a mania for obscure and opaque words whose true meaning is known only to the select few — those ritually selected under our first point.

It all adds up to a rather unpalatable product whose utility as a means of conveying information or even advancing scholarship may legitimately be questioned. That there is some contribution, some benefit, no one would deny. But it is less than it might be, because the constituencies served are tiny, and the outside audience or readership — outside the professions, that is — is slight.[13]

Can anything be done? There are suggestions. Bronwyn Drainie, whose attempt to bridge the gap between literacy and scholarship we described earlier, had a simple solution. Why not publish most scholarly books and journals on the Internet, a vehicle readily available to those who take an interest in such things?

It is an elegant idea, well within the reach of contemporary technology. The mechanisms are there and familiarity with electronic information retrieval is increasing. It has the advantage that it would spare acres of trees, perhaps whole forests. Others have had the same thought. At the end of 1996 there were 1700 electronic journals up and running, and their number had doubled within the previous year. Better still, anxious authors could get their articles accepted or rejected within three months, compared with the average of two years for clogged print journals.[14]

---

13. This observation is aimed at the humanities and social sciences; the sciences occupy a different pond, with a more active interchange among professional species.

14. AUCC–CARL, "The Changing World of Scholarly Communication."

There are drawbacks, too. If libraries are crowded, so is the Internet. We would be transferring drivel from one sector to another, where the guideposts, and the ability to scan and select, are still primitive. Anyone who has dredged through the acres of real estate ads and egotistical home pages that are the backbone of the Internet will know that this particular technology is having growing pains and that it furnishes only an incomplete answer to an important question. It is practical, but so far it is the intellectual equivalent of establishing a red-light district in answer to the problem of prostitution — out of sight of most, and out of mind.

The Internet is like a vast library that started off with its books jumbled together and without catalogues. Guidebooks immediately sprouted, cruise directors set up shop, and technical shortcuts were devised to ease the pain of navigating the electronic sea. The advantages the Internet confers in access to information are not only indisputable but overwhelming. Statistics Canada data, the *Washington Post* (updated every half hour), the Department of Foreign Affairs in Ottawa attract readers to the electronic library and even, possibly, the electronic bookshop.

True, it is a library where anybody can walk in off the street and place her or his book on the shelves. There is no real cure for this problem, as early attempts at Internet censorship seem to have demonstrated. The bulk will eventually defeat itself — and is already doing so. Bookmarks and automatic Web sites are the first stage of selection; paid access to privileged ("published") information may be the second.

So, besides adopting the Drainie forest conservation program, we would suggest something else. Ease the pressure on academics to publish quantity and focus them on quality.[15] Retreat from specialization

---

15. Others have had the same idea. The AUCC–CARL task force on Academic Libraries and Scholarly Communication concluded in 1996 that "universities [should] debate the relationship between the academic reward structure and the publishing activities of scholars and explore the possibility of implementing other reward models that focus on the quality rather than the quantity of publications."

and dismantle some, if not all, of the professional rituals that enjoin pointless publication. It's true that these changes would be a strain. There would be more pressure on academics to read the fewer (many fewer, we hope) books and articles that would be published, on paper or on the Internet. Those professors choosing to stay on in the universities might even discuss their colleagues' works and openly say whether they are good or bad. They would no longer feel a compulsion to be professionally indifferent. And in abandoning some of their professional obsessions, they might actually do something to save their profession.

Chapter 8

How to Choose a University:
What to Expect from a University Education

CHOOSING A UNIVERSITY ranks up there with marriage, getting hired, and buying a house as one of the more important decisions people can make in the course of their lives. Once started in university, the decisions keep coming: not merely where to go, but how to pay, what to do when you get there, and what to do afterwards. There are guides to law, business, and graduate schools. The "how-to" sections of bookstores are crammed with manuals, while public libraries overflow with advice.

And such advice! *The Truth about College and How to Survive and Succeed as a Student* is one, which competes with *The Real Guide to Canadian Universities* and *The M&S Guide to Ontario's Colleges of Applied Arts and Technology*. There is the *Complete Book of Colleges* (with free CD-ROM) and *The Best 310 Colleges. Manage Your Time*, one title warns, in competition with several other practical compendiums.

Getting into college at all is a primary question, and one that many writers are happy to answer. They are helped, in most places, by the absence of standard school-leaving exams. *How to Prepare for Canadian University Entrance Exams in . . .* is quite specific. More general, and more American, are *Acing the New SAT* [Scholastic Aptitude Test] and *Barron's Basic Tips on the SAT*. There is also *The SAT for Dummies* and *The Young Woman's Guide to Better SAT Scores: Fighting the Gender Gap*. Those worrying about the SAT may already be thinking of themselves in an American context: to help prepare for their future there is *The International Student's Guide to Going to College in America*. The resourceful need not rely only on exams, however. *Write Your Way Into College* advises another author; *Composing a Successful Application*. For the desperate, there is *College Admission: Cracking the System*. For those who cannot survive on athletic scholarships, there is *The Debt-Free Graduate: How to Survive College or University without Going Broke*. For those who favour distance education, there is a guide to make the airwaves or the phone lines their very own.

The general universities section of one large Canadian public (not university) library boasts no fewer than 140 books on the subject, which does not include the forty-two specifically Canadian books on universities and the university experience. If all books in the university category were added together, it would — at that library — total around four hundred, and that, of course, is only a fraction of what is generally available in English, worldwide. Specialists are another matter: like other categories of academics they drone on infinitely, but, as we have suggested elsewhere, their books are not usually read, merely printed.

The best-known guide in Canada is *Maclean's* annual ranking of Canadian universities. It originally appeared as a regular issue of the magazine and proved immensely popular. Now in stiffer covers, it has become the universities' equivalent of the *Dogs' Own Annual*, sought by customers and fanciers of all kinds. *Maclean's* annual rankings of universities appealed to the counting spirit — rather like the Ten Best-Dressed Men or Women, or the Most Liveable City in Canada. The least that can be said of *Maclean's* is that it found a market niche; as some universities darkly suspect, it probably is a factor in university selection.

The books, the guides, and *Maclean's* are only information in the very traditional medium of print. Why, after all, go to a library, when information is just a few taps away? Universities have enthusiastically adopted the Internet as a medium of propaganda. They have their Web sites and home pages that detail their history and their prospects, with better examples of their architecture and portraits of their photogenic professors. For those who prefer to sit back for twenty minutes and let the information roll, colleges and universities have special video cassettes.

Admission anxieties in Canada have not gone as far as in the United States. There, would-be applicants can hire counsellors to prepare them for the arduous admissions process. In some cases, American students start working with counsellors in grade 11, selecting the right courses and preparing the appropriate profile. In a competitive world, most services can be bought, from advice to editing to authorship.

Most of this activity is harmless, and some may actually be constructive. It keeps computer programmers in funds and it helps pay the bills of the mellifluous announcers who are hired to tout one seat of learning or another. In a consumer society, the buyer is presumed to know enough to beware.

Many of the guides give advice on how scarce (and therefore desirable) a product may be. Admission to Queen's University, for example, is rated more difficult than admission to the University of Toronto. Admission to either (56% success at Toronto, 52% at Queen's, according to the Princeton Review's *Complete Book of Colleges*) is much easier than, for example, admission to Harvard (10%). Something so desirable, so much in demand as Harvard suggests that simply getting there is its own reward. "Harvard is like a generic term," one American student quipped. "Like Kleenex."[1]

Why does a Canadian book cite Harvard? Not because Harvard necessarily gives its undergraduates an incomparable education — it doesn't — but because it enjoys brand recognition in Canada as it does in the United States. Canadian high school graduates increasingly view the border with the United States as irrelevant to their careers and futures, certainly as compared with the advantages that the "brand" confers on them.

The advice offered in these guides does not always match what people want to know or should know. And it is less certain whether advice rendered today based on past experience or even on what currently

---

1. Quoted in Bruce Weber, "Inside the Meritocracy Machine," *New York Times Magazine*, 28 April 1996, 46.

exists will be appropriate four or five years from now. A university education is and always has been something of a gamble. At certain times and in certain places, and depending on the objective sought, it is possible to improve the odds. But not always.

There are many reasons for enrolling at a university. There are general trends: for example, many more women today feel the call to higher education, reflecting a major change in society's values and priorities over the last generation or two. It may be accurate, if not consoling, to gaze at an individual and suggest that, after all, she is just part of a large statistical pattern. Yet in terms of fulfilling society's expectations, or her friends' behaviour, or her parents' deferred ambitions, that is very often the case.

It may be piety that drives enrolment, it may be family, it may be personal obsessions, or any number of things. But suppose, as a 1992 survey did, that it boils down to four objectives: general self-improvement, in-depth knowledge of a field of study, improved chances of a good income, and acquisition of job skills.[2] Take the question of the link between university and employment, or education and income. This question is seldom distant from the thoughts of students and their relatives. It is perhaps the question most frequently asked by students, and most frequently evaded by professors. This is because, while there are some answers to the question, they are not entirely satisfactory, and professors are understandably reluctant to voice them. And that is as good a place to begin as any.

———

Jobs. Let us start with some abstractions which, because they are conveyed in numbers and are called statistics, seem to be magically solid and reliable. In 1995, Canadians with higher education were more

---

2. Warren Clark, "Attitudes of Bachelor's Graduates towards Their Programs," *Education Quarterly Review* 1, 2 (1994): 10–30.

likely employed (91.2%) than those with merely high school completion (83.8%) or, heaven forbid, those with eight years or less of schooling (59%). Moreover, they had a higher income than Canadians without higher education.

Income increases with educational attainment, too. Lucky holders of a bachelor's degree made, on the average, $35,000 a year in 1991 if they had graduated in 1986 in the social sciences, and $41,000 for the same year's graduates in engineering. Possession of a master's degree boosted the engineers to $50,000 and the social scientists to $42,000. If they attained the summit of a PhD, the rate of increase slowed for engineers, to $55,000, but picked up in the social sciences, to $50,000. The same tale, with variations, applied across a variety of fields, from humanities (lowest) to commerce (highest), which in a neo-conservative age is doubtless as it should be.

Why is there this correlation between increasing education and increasing pay, jobs, and social status? Is it because the more education (learning) one has, the better one performs? Or could it be that the process of getting into, and out of, a university performs a useful, or at any rate inevitable, sorting function, quite independent of what one learns? Education trains, but it also sorts.

The association between higher education and higher income is easy to make. In many senses there is a direct relationship. Qualifications for job applicants have increased steadily over time, while within organizations further education or professionalization, or other forms of training, are usually systematically rewarded. BA, MA, PhD — the trend is up.

Is it the education or the credential that is being rewarded? That is a chicken-and-egg question. The one signifies the other, in theory and usually in practice. You cannot be a member of certain professions without the appropriate diploma — you cannot be a medical doctor without an MD, and you cannot, usually, be a lawyer without an LLB. Of course, if you have an MD or an LLB, you are not condemned to be a doctor or a lawyer, and there have always been some individuals who have kicked over their professional traces and grazed, happily, elsewhere.

University professors without PhDs or other doctorates are very uncommon; these days it is hard to get in the door without one. Sometimes other, rare, qualifications suffice: Harvard thinks it is enough for someone to be, say, an ex–prime minister of Canada to qualify for temporary employment, while the University of Toronto has been known to accept ex-premiers on an ongoing basis.

The credential does not always suffice. Some readers may remember a time when teaching jobs were in surplus and teachers in short supply. Time was when the term "unemployed lawyer" was an oxymoron, rather like "bald sheep." Aspiring lawyers do not anticipate becoming unemployed, and they do not expect to become poor. But some are unemployed, and some do become poor. Going by the averages, they have a good chance to be neither, but the trend of unemployment is up, and incomes have stalled at roughly their 1970 level. Increasingly, there are stories of lawyers packing up their degrees and heading off to meet their destiny as qualified teachers of English as a Second Language in Korea.

There may soon be too many doctors; some, looking at our soaring health costs, argue that there already are. Granted, doctors are not always in the right place at the right time. Doctors have had more portable skills than other professionals — the ability to pack themselves and their degrees off to the land of milk and money, the United States. Yet recent trends suggest that medical mobility may be becoming a thing of the past, and that medical schools too are producing too many qualified physicians for the economy to absorb. There are even reports from the United States that American doctors may find themselves regulated into lower salaries and lower social status — fortunately by the Market, and not by the monster of Big Government.

What does experience show for the non-professionals, the undergraduates? According to a Statistics Canada survey of 1992 graduates with a bachelor's degree, respondents "reported the largest gap between their expectations and the results [of their education] in the area of the acquisition of job skills." For some, and probably for many, this did not matter. Humanities graduates did not expect to acquire job skills by studying literature or philosophy or history, and by and large they got what they expected. Education graduates, on the other hand, tended to be disappointed. Expecting much, they got some of what they expected, practical training, without much of a place to practise in the job climate of the early 1990s. They might just as well have opted for the impracticalities of history.[3]

It is not that students are taking a purposeful detour, a prolonged furlough from reality. Our Statscan survey indicates that the vast majority (82%) of university graduates would prefer to be employed in or near their field of study. In the case of humanists, this preference is tempered by a realization that jobs are less likely: in the sober words of the statisticians, "More than half the humanities graduates said their program provided them with little or no knowledge of career opportunities in their field."[4]

Does university training confer a knowledge of job opportunities? In co-op programs (where work experience and education are combined), and in health and engineering, yes. Elsewhere, not really or not at all.

Doctors and lawyers, teachers and professors, humanists and social scientists — these are only illustrations of how changeable the job market has been and may be, and how quickly today's sure thing becomes tomorrow's redundancy. Rigid expectations, that jobs and higher education must march in happy lock-step into a prosperous future, are in fact a curious variant of an old-fashioned idea of rigorous planning — curious because proponents of the notion are often associated with a narrow and doctrinaire devotion to the notion of the market. "Marketable skills," "job credentials," "learning by doing," and similar forms of verbal nonsense actually assume a level of knowledge and predictability that as mere historians we would shy away from — except to venture that our scepticism is more practically based than the blind optimism of the proponents of "education-as-marketplace."

---

3. Ibid., 16.
4. Ibid., 26.

But what about the connection between higher income and higher learning? It's there, but the wrong conclusions have been drawn from it. We are inclined to think that it is the credential rather than the essence of knowledge that determines the level of reward, and that as supply outstrips demand the value assigned to the credential will likewise decline.

This is not to deny that university-educated people are better qualified and more capable than those lacking such a degree or two or three. It is at least possible, and in our opinion highly probable, that this is so because bright, active, energetic and imaginative people gravitate to universities and that universities ratify rather than confer these qualities. Bright and active people are more likely than others to find jobs and create opportunities, but the relationship between their university education and their future employment is more indirect than is generally supposed.

———

Educational satisfaction. More Canadians than ever before (15% of the population between ages 25 and 64) have been to university. What do they think of their experience? Have the universities created a satisfied clientele? If we are to judge from what members of the federal Cabinet had to say about universities when they considered how, or whether, to fund universities, the answer is "apparently not." If we consider the numbers of students continuing to flow into universities generation after generation, and incurring debt in the process, the answer is "apparently yes." As between debt and taxes, the truth is somewhere in between.

Satisfaction with education is often measured institution by institution. We don't deny that this is important, but there are other kinds of measurement. According to the counters at Statscan, 86 percent of 1990 graduates queried were "satisfied or very satisfied with the quality of teaching in their program." Teaching quality was just one of the criteria used. There were also faculty availability, institutional facilities (laboratories, libraries, and the like), and class size.

Breaking down responses by fields, Canada is a country of happy humanists, and slightly jaundiced engineers and agronomists. Social scientists also ranked their experience below the national average. It is tempting to conclude that the more impractical — the less job related — the field, the higher the satisfaction experienced by universities' student-clients.

Equally interesting is how Canadian graduates assessed the development of their skills as part of their university experience. "Independent thinking" was ranked most highly — highest in the humanities and fine arts, and lowest in education. "Decision making" was next, this time with graduates of the health sciences reporting the best results as they prepared to take those life-and-death decisions characteristic of their career choice. Education again ranked low. Then "good writing skills," which evoked the warmest response from humanities graduates, and the worst from business faculties. Future business men and women also ranked themselves low in "good speaking skills," though not as low as mathematicians and engineers. These are self-rankings, and we are struck by how closely these data conform to traditional stereotypes.[5]

Clearly, Canadian graduates had some reservations about their university experience. Some felt they had not learned to express themselves, while others believed they had not matured sufficiently — making choices or thinking independently. Yet almost all — 96 percent — would do it again. Not quite 80 percent would select the same university if they had to do it over, and 69.7 percent would choose the same field. Using this last criterion, students of biology or life sciences were least satisfied, followed closely by social scientists, general arts and science students, and humanists. Health, education, and fine arts led the satisfaction parade: given the choice, over three-quarters of graduates in these areas would repeat the experience.[6]

---

5. Ibid., 19, table 4.
6. Ibid., 19, 29–30.

How much is enough? Part 1: Paying for it all. If there is still a connection between university education and jobs and income, and if recent university graduates report a fair degree of satisfaction with their experience, it may not seem unreasonable to decide in favour of going to university. How much should a student, or a student's family, pay for the privilege?

Until recently the answer to that question was very little. The exigencies of university finance in the 1990s suggest otherwise, however. Tuition is on the way up.

We do not wish to be alarmist. Tuition fees, measured in constant dollars, are in the mid-1990s *below* where they were in the early 1960s.[7] For much of that thirty-year stretch, Canadian incomes were rising very steadily and impressively, further reducing the burden on students and their families. For thirty years students have enjoyed an education discounted in cash terms. On the other hand, there were far fewer students in the early 1960s than there are today, and government policy has been directed at increasing the proportion of Canadians attending university.

Universities have not taken the road to tuition increases without considerable misgivings. Some are doctrinaire: university education is assumed to be a public good, and there are those who assume it not only ought to be, but must be, available to everybody. Some are prudential: each $100 increase in tuition, it is argued, reduces the available pool of students by 1 percent. Unless one assumes a perfect match between brains and wealth and merit — which historical experience suggests is risky — higher tuition might possibly result in a more challenging student body for academics to teach.[8]

---

7. Council of Ontario Universities, *The Financial Position of Universities in Ontario: 1995* (May 1995), figure 27.

8. The *Globe and Mail* disagrees. In an editorial titled "Higher Tuition Could Mean Better Access," 22 September 1995, the *Globe* argues that a deregulated tuition system would "establish a market, allowing students to be more discriminating in choosing where to attend. ... The result of all this? Empowered students. Self-sufficient universities. Higher-quality education. A stronger work force. A more prosperous country."

Tuition fees, ultimately, are set by how much, and how, the public thinks it should pay. Up till now, the public has preferred to pay through plentiful tax dollars channelled to universities through provincial governments. In the late 1990s, governments wish to pay less, which means that someone else will pay more — in this case, the student.

The model is at hand — the United States. In that country, student expenses at public and private institutions rose by more than 100 percent between 1984 and 1994. It is possible that Canadian costs will follow a similar trajectory as governments offload their costs.

Let us assume that Canadian tuition will rise to the level of tuition at the better American state (not private) universities. This is a safe assumption, because in some areas it has already happened. Fees for would-be dentists, or doctors of pharmacy at the nation's largest university, Toronto, have already reached or surpassed comparable American charges. Other fields — undergraduate and graduate studies in arts and sciences, medicine, and masters of business administration — are still notably lower than their American counterparts. MBA fees, for example, could expect to double; undergraduate fees would grow by a third; and MDs would see their tuition rise by about 250 percent. We expect to see this happen, in progressive steps, over the next few years. Anyone considering postponing or deferring university study might wish to take this probability into account.

How would this increase be paid for? The short answer is out of family pocketbooks, and then out of loans. It is improbable that scholarships will increase sufficiently to cover increased tuition. They will increase some, certainly, and not everybody even under the new, more costly dispensation will be disadvantaged. But they will not, they cannot, increase enough.

Again the American example, though not prescriptive, is instructive. As costs were rising in the 1984–94 period by over 100 percent, funds for student aid also increased — by 60 percent. This was a period of rather less acute financial stringency in the United States than we are now experiencing in Canada. The forms of student aid also changed in the United States in this period — more loans and fewer grants.

There are differences aplenty between the United States and Canada, but the resemblances are compelling. For example, in both countries family incomes have been stagnating or declining. Savings rates have been dropping steadily since the early 1980s, and consumer debt, as the media never cease to remind us, is high. The percentage of family income that will have to be dedicated to tuition fees has risen and will rise. Increased tuition costs will thus prove a heavier burden than they would have five or twenty years ago, and the burden will be deferred, in the form of debt.

Loans are nothing new. There have always been loans to cover university education. The Canada Student Loan program, in existence for more than thirty years, gave students access to funds through a federal guarantee of bank loans. Canada's banks, presented with a riskless and profitable proposition, were happy to hand over the money and to bill Ottawa for the defaults. A student loan scheme, as we have seen, was a major part of human resources minister Lloyd Axworthy's attempt to revise university funding in 1994–95.

In a growing economy, a student loan scheme had much to recommend it. In the shrinking economy of the 1990s, with scarce jobs paying lower returns, the Canada Student Loan scheme harvested record bankruptcies: $70 million, the highest total ever, was recorded in 1995-96; $277 million since 1990. The same thing happened to provincial programs, such as Ontario's OSAP, which in 1995 paid out $35 million on defaulted student loans.[9]

Not surprisingly, the government decided to shrink the load, just as it was doing in other fields, by transferring some of the risk to the banks. Instead of an absolute guarantee of repayment, Ottawa now pays Canadian banks a "risk premium," which encourages them to pursue their debtors with much more vigour than was the case under the older, easier arrangements. There are in any case more loans

---

9. Elaine Carey, "Today's Grads: Forever Young, Forever Bankrupt," *Toronto Star*, 14 November 1996.

because Canadian governments, like their American cousins, have been trying to get out of the grant business. What was once a mixture of loans and grants is now, ideally and in fact, all loans. This burden falls on the "McJob" generation, whose opportunities for quick, well-paid employment are less than those of previous generations. In one case, cited in the press, a mathematics graduate struggled to repay a $30,000 student loan debt out of a part-time job at a restaurant. Not surprisingly, she couldn't.

"They go bankrupt because they have no choice," one bankruptcy trustee was quoted as saying. "They end up being harassed by collection agencies — and harassed is not too strong a word — and sometimes they really have no choice."[10]

The student debt load has been getting heavier, and shows signs of getting heavier still. Sixty percent of full-time students now borrow from the Canada Student Loan Program at some point. Their debt load was an average of $8700 in 1990, and a 1997 study projected that it will triple by 1998 — higher, at least for undergraduates, than Australia or the United States.[11] A $25,000 debt might well be greater than a typical graduate's income for the first few years of employment and might, at some point, prove an effective deterrent to university enrolment.

In these circumstances another idea of the 1980s, loan repayments tied to income level, has taken on a new attraction. Student loans would be repaid as and when the debtor can afford to pay them off. If the debtor is unemployed, or holding down a McJob, repayments would be little or nil. On the other hand, if the debtor prospers, the loan repayments increase because the means to repay them is at hand, and affordable. This notion was floated by Lloyd Axworthy in his university

---

10. Ibid.

11. "Canadian Students Most Indebted in World," *University of Toronto Bulletin,* 3 March 1997, citing *Reviewing Student Assistance,* a study just released by the AUCC (Association of Universities and Colleges of Canada), CAUT (Canadian Association of University Teachers), and national student groups.

finance excursion and it won some support, though not enough to save his scheme.

Income-contingent loans have the great advantage that they are tied to something concrete. Existing student loan schemes are a gamble, based on inadequate if not defective assumptions. Because repayment of a loan does not begin for four or five years or more after the date of the loan, it is next to impossible to predict what conditions an individual student debtor will face when the loan comes due. Under income-contingency, a student will know one thing for sure: repayment of the debt will be tied to ability to pay.

There are admittedly other ways to look at the problem. True to provincial form, an Ontario government official put a different spin on government approval of income-contingent loans. Tying loans to the income tax system, this official gloated to a reporter, would mean that "the only people who could default would be those who vanished and escaped.[12] We can see the slogan now, and catchy it is: "Indenture or Emigration — the Common Sense Solution." If this come-on for a university education is widely adopted by governments, students may well look for a cheaper and less onerous form of study than this little political gift that keeps on giving.

There is another solution under income-contingent loans — earning nothing at all. Certainly for those who expect to be unemployed, or who expect to join some kind of monastic order, this is the way to go.

Tying loan repayment to income tax — to a progressive income tax is plainly what is meant — means the creation of a kind of education surtax. The administrative attractions of such a scheme are obvious. The mechanisms already exist, the principles are well understood, and evasion is difficult, though not absolutely impossible. If tax rates are kept reasonably low, at any rate lower than they have been, the burden

12. Quoted ibid.; it is also a view welcomed by editorialists of the *Globe and Mail*: "Higher Tuition Could Mean Better Access," 22 September 1995: "Collection would come through the tax system, which would reduce the fraud and delinquency of the current program."

may not be too great. On the other hand, like income tax, and as Canadians have seen in their politics over the past five years, another surtax may well become a political liability. Thus the optics, and the linkage to the existing tax system, will have to be carefully managed or, just possibly, concealed.

Income-contingent loans, then, are not a perfect solution from the consumer's point of view. They are, however, fairer than any other idea currently on the market, and they have the edge in terms of affordability and predictability. Granted, they do not offer the escape-hatch of bankruptcy, but governments are in any case moving to narrow access to bankruptcy for ex-students.

In the final analysis, income-contingent loans will work, and can work, only if Canadian tuition has a ceiling. We have suggested that the ceiling is roughly the level of the good American state schools — Michigan or California. Canadian education will cease to be the bargain it is and has been, but it will continue to be within the reach of the middle class.

———————

How much is enough? Part 2: BAs, MAs, and PhDs and where to find them. To someone entering university for the first time, a Bachelor of Arts may seem like an impossibly long commitment, its achievement an almost infinite time away.

Let's assume the best. Your background is adequate, your courses sufficiently interesting, your passage relatively smooth. Time passes quickly — three, four, or five years' time — and then you have to consider the next stage. Is a BA enough? Put another way, Is a BA what it once was?

It certainly doesn't do what it once did. A BA, or a BSc, or a BComm, or any of the other first-level degrees, once opened doors to employment: stable, secure, perhaps lifetime employment. That was a generation, and another economy, ago. There are fewer such jobs today, and far fewer in relation to the number of BAs available to fill them.

This is, of course, the result of deliberate government policy. In Canada, the United States, and elsewhere, governments have expanded the number of degree-granting institutions. Margaret Thatcher's Britain, to take one example, conferred degree-granting powers on the polytechnics, with instantly gratifying results in terms of the number and proportion of Britons with university degrees. The BA, being a more plentiful commodity, is now worth less, in terms of jobs, money, and security.

A BA *plus* something else — the right school, the right background, an extra degree or two — suddenly that becomes enough. Thatcher's Britain was a pretty "robust" place, to use the current government and media jargon signifying approval. The Iron Lady did more than multiply BAs with a wave of her parliamentary majority. She created a multi-tiered post-secondary education system, with universities obliged to compete for resources that were suddenly much scarcer. More than that: she decreed that professors seeking promotion would abandon tenure in order to compete for the new job; and their old jobs would similarly be thrown open to competition.

Thatcher's educational reforms recognized that Great Britain could not afford to pay for a system in which scores of degree-granting institutions each pretended to be Oxford, London, or Cambridge. Money therefore went to reinforce strength, strength being directed into research departments, institutes, and universities. In our concentration on our American cousins, we sometimes forget that there are other English-speaking countries, from Britain to New Zealand, and that their post-secondary practices are not entirely irrelevant. This is especially the case with Great Britain, where Thatcher's achievements and example are greatly admired by Canadian small-c conservatives.

The division between first- and second- and possibly even third-tier universities is not new to Canada. Canada has large and larger universities, with faculties that are generally admitted to be weak or strong or somewhere in between. There is already a Group of Ten Canadian universities that see themselves in size or talent or both as being the nation's first-class institutions. These are UBC, Alberta,

McMaster, Western Ontario, Toronto, Waterloo, Queen's, McGill, Montréal, and Laval. There is even a fear that UBC, Toronto, and Queen's see themselves as a smaller Group of Three, with interests even more specialized than the Group of Ten.

What does this have to do with choice of a university? Something, though not everything. Let us consider the positive case first. Plainly, there are even now post-secondary institutions in Canada with larger resources and larger aspirations than others. Full-service institutions today, they are the Canadian universities most likely to be full-service institutions tomorrow. Their working conditions, including course load and salary, to some extent already reflect this status; these institutions would have to travel further along this road. Better working conditions attract better faculty, and better faculty create more prestige. More prestige, a better brand name, in turn attracts students, or so the thinking goes. And better students in turn satisfy the good faculty, creating a cycle of satisfaction.

As we indicated earlier, Canadian universities do not exist in isolation, either from universities in other countries or from competing educational services. As things stand, Canadian universities are best known for their cheapness in relation to the quality of their product. With tuition fees rising, they will lose part of their competitive edge — low cost — compared with good American state schools. This prospect suggests that Canadian universities and their government sponsors should concentrate on beefing up those institutions that have a chance to compete internationally.

The case for attending a university with a strong faculty, strong services, and, perhaps most important, a competitive brand name, is persuasive. Students seeking breadth of subject matter and depth of faculty resources should consider the Big Ten or the Big Three universities first; so should students seeking to graduate with a degree from an institution whose rank and standing are generally, meaning internationally, recognized.

That said, this happy rational model isn't always how students choose universities. Any parent of a university-bound teenager knows this truth. Take the consideration of faculty prestige. It isn't exactly an item you can take to your neighbourhood bank. Academic awards, fellowships, university-press books — these accomplishments count for almost nothing to an above-average seventeen year old. What if a faculty member wins a Nobel Prize? These events are reported in the media, and for a few cheerful hours the host institution for the happy prize-winner bathes in the resulting publicity. But does it translate? This is not a question much studied in Canada, where there are only three living Nobel prizewinners, all scientists, of whom two currently teach in Canadian universities. Have the University of Toronto and the University of British Columbia secured students as a result? Possibly on the graduate level; but as for undergraduates, it is more than doubtful.[13]

More relevant for many students are social considerations. We do not disparage these criteria. They count, they are important, and they have always been part of the university experience. Getting away from home is part of the ritual of growing up, and university falls at the right point in people's lives for such an event. Experiencing someplace different — but perhaps not too different — is important, too. Feelings of community, companionship, friendship matter as well. If such sentiments are mixed as they sometimes are with small institutions and small classes, students can benefit exponentially. That is the theory, and sometimes it actually works. But we should observe that few of Canada's smaller colleges have the same reputation as their American competitors — Amherst, Bard, Oberlin, Reed, and the rest. Perhaps with the passage of time, with imagination and innovation, they will, but as yet we do not see it. More than at the big schools, this is where financial stringency is biting most deeply, reducing an already diminished

13. See the aptly titled article in the *New York Times*, 9 June 1996: "College A or B? It All Depends, Sometimes: News, Good or Bad, Can Influence Choice of Applicants. Maybe." One bemused professor is quoted as saying: "I would like to say that students come to us because of the quality of our intellectual life. But let's face it, athletics is the coin of the realm." The reputation of college athletic teams is apparently the one sure predictor for student applications to various American schools.

capacity to compete. Yet because overhead is less, and buildings and faculty fewer, the game is not completely lost. Not yet.

All of which brings us back to where we started, with printed guides, Web sites, and promotional videos masking a state of change and uncertainty in Canada's universities. The universities' uncertainties mirror those of society at large. Will Canada and Canadian institutions falter in international competition and fail seriously to compete in a globalized world? If so, then Canadian students would be best advised to seek the American model, either directly by going to the United States, or indirectly by applying to the closest Canadian imitation of an American school. If not, Canada still has a strenuous if not arduous path ahead; and so do Canada's students.

A *Cri de Coeur*:
A Call for Change

WE WROTE *THE GREAT BRAIN ROBBERY* in the early 1980s as a wake-up call to our colleagues, to the general public, to students, and to politicians. We thought that Canada's universities had kept all the bad habits they had picked up in the turbulent 1960s and had learned nothing new since then. We believed that if things continued on as they were, Canada's universities would stay on the road to ruin.

Canadian higher education is in much better shape today than it was fifteen years ago, but then Canada is, for the most part, in better shape also. Most Canadian universities now recognize the crucial importance of research not only in generating revenues for themselves but in earning much-needed dollars in cooperation with the private sector in their local communities. They are also much more willing to acknowledge that teaching and research are interconnected and that research adds content to teaching at all levels.

Still, our universities' internal budgeting is lagging behind the demands that students and the public are putting on them for more relevant content and more flexible programs of study. Almost without exception, universities still distribute the vast bulk of their budget dollars to faculties and departments that act as fiefdoms, rather than as parts of an integrated whole. While the demand for inter- and cross-disciplinary studies grows at universities across Canada, such programs are still a tiny minority of what is offered.

Knowledge is being increasingly integrated in the real world, but universities still treat knowledge as nothing more than the sum of its parts, primarily because it is easier to budget that way. When the time comes that a faculty member is treated in the budgeting process as a member of a larger university community, rather than as a "full-time equivalent" in a particular department, then the real potential of inter- and cross-disciplinary studies may be reached. For the most part, that time has not yet come.

We also believe that students today ought to be better than they were a decade ago, because the universities have raised their entrance requirements. At some universities the students are of higher calibre; at others, there has been no improvement and possibly even a decline. As we argued, the high schools have pushed their grades ever higher to keep pace with university entrance requirements. This is bad enough but, worse yet, they have not done a good job of preparing students for university. It's not just the school's fault, of course. Years of watching television instead of reading, or surfing the net instead of thinking, appear to have lowered the learning capacity of a whole generation of students. This decline amounts to a national disaster in the making, for a nation without good universities cannot function at its capacity in the information age. It is also a personal tragedy for students who scrimp and save to go to university only to drop out, or to graduate without ever learning how to read, analyse, write, and think.

Canada is in the midst of a revolution in public values no less pro- found than the onrush towards social welfare that began in the closing months of the Second World War. At that time, Canadians developed their mindset to "let government do it." In the intervening years we lost track of the real costs of government and, as a result, ended up in unbearable debt. The current revolution results from the damage that mindset caused. Most Canadians are rediscovering the virtues of thrift, self-reliance, and hard work. We are curing our profligate ways and starting to build a society based on realistic expectations of national wealth and future performance. We are cutting up our national credit cards and learning to pay our way.

Today's universities are also more fiscally responsible than those of the past few years. They have learned the hard way that taxpayer dollars are not to be used frivolously and that they themselves must put more effort into building solid, healthy financial foundations. With some notable exceptions (McGill University, with its continuing high debt, is the best example we can think of), universities have responded positively to the public's demand for financial accountability. The lesson that they must conserve resources is sinking in.

Canada's universities were not eager to join this revolution, but they have had little choice in the matter. They have had to cut back staff, trim facility budgets, and charge more for tuition and for various public services they perform. Although Canadian university tuitions are still, on average, lower than those in the United States, they are climbing rapidly and will soon reach a rough parity with U.S. state universities.

The fee revolution has affected students in various ways. The current generation did not expect to run into this growing barrier to higher education. After all, for most of the last three decades, a university education was cheap in Canada because of heavy taxpayer subsidies. That is no longer true, but students in universities have had little time to prepare for the change. In the United States, where fees have been substantially higher for much longer, the middle classes long ago ceased to take heavy taxpayer subsidies for granted. Unlike their Canadian counterparts, they knew that preparing to have Sally go to university meant putting money away from the time she was born. The next generation of Canadians who aspire to university will know that, too.

In the meantime, many students amass large debts before they graduate. One reason (aside from the tuition increases) is that Canadian universities pour hundreds of millions of dollars into scholarship funds (ostensibly distributed on the basis of merit), but comparatively little into bursaries, which are given out on the basis of merit *and* need. Another is that governments have taken very little of the money they have saved through cutbacks and directed it into low-cost, long-term loans.

At the same time that universities have come under increasing budget pressures from cutbacks, they are also being scrutinized more closely by the general public and by governments. That, we think, is a good thing and is bound to lead to a higher-quality university degree.

As the voting public gets better educated itself, it is coming to realize that universities are important national assets that cannot simply be allowed to drift along. Alberta is leading the way in developing specific performance indicators for its universities; other governments will surely follow. And although the *Maclean's* survey still leaves much to be desired, universities ignore it at their peril.

———————

Canadian universities are being challenged as never before by other forms of post-secondary education, public and private, and are beginning to awaken to the challenge. Most universities have little internal flexibility, because their budgets remain dominated by the salaries of tenured professors, so they are forced to be innovative in the methods they use to deliver education. This challenge is invigorating, and more flexibility is needed in the delivery of distance education and in degree requirements. At the same time, however, universities must not succumb to faddishness. Their prime mission is still to teach people how to think, and a basic liberal arts education remains the soundest way to do that. Concordia University and Carleton University are two that have tried to refocus attention on liberal arts education; all universities in this country must follow their example.

Although many things in the world of Canadian universities are better, or hold greater promise, than they did a decade ago, some things are unimproved, or worse. Despite all the brave words of politicians in Ontario, Alberta, and elsewhere, tenure is as entrenched as ever. This is ironic, because tenure is less needed than ever. Provincial and federal human rights legislation, collective agreements (union and non-union), and mission statements adopted by virtually every university in Canada hold out the ideal of the free search for knowledge and the protection of the right to dissent. Academic freedom has never had so many protective devices as it does today. Yet tenure thrives. No one, it seems, is willing to take it on.

If the granting of tenure were only a practice engaged in for the protection of academic freedom, we would accept it. But it is not. It is a virtual guarantee of job security and, worse, it has frozen the demographic profile of the Canadian university teaching profession as it was in the late 1960s. This entrenchment has had a particularly negative impact on the gender profile of the university teaching profession in Canada.

Everywhere in Canada, women are beginning to swell the number of degree holders in programs that were once the exclusive province of men. They are in an absolute majority among all university undergraduates today and they are beginning to earn large numbers of advanced degrees in fields such as engineering, where they were once a tiny minority. But they are not even approaching a large minority of tenured university professors, despite all the affirmative hiring action programs that universities have mounted in the past decade. Why? Because of tenure. Abolish tenure, or at least abolish tenure as job security, and thousands of these women (and recently graduated men) will be able to rush in to replace those professors who ought not to be on the public payroll any longer.

Universities in Canada today face grave danger from those who would throttle academic freedom in the name of political correctness. In some ways, we admit, it is easy to appreciate the anger of such zealots, for sometimes specific research projects appear to play into their hands. We have already declared that we cannot judge the scientific validity of psychologist J. Philippe Rushton's research into racial differences, but we can understand why some faculty and students are angry with him. Nonetheless, Rushton is a distinguished scholar with an impressive track record who has done nothing illegal. Indeed, his critics — shouting him down and attempting to eject him from the university — have acted with appalling crudity, boorishness, and stupidity. The anger of those who shout loudly must not be permitted to stifle research or to stamp out debate on campus. Those who oppose Rushton's research findings or those of any other controversial scholar should challenge them openly in scholarly journals and in public debate; if they are correct, their arguments will make the case.

If such research is fraudulent, the university that harbours it ought to deal with the miscreant. But a university must not take action against a teacher or a researcher simply because a question is being posed that leaves others uncomfortable, or even makes them angry. Universities must remain among the very few places on earth where the unconventional, the uncomfortable, the once unmentionable can be pursued in both teaching and research. A university must be an open and free marketplace for all manner of opinions. The book in which Hitler outlined his plan for war and the annihilation of the Jews, *Mein Kampf*, must have a place on every university library book shelf. So must the fraudulent works of Holocaust deniers and other outright racists. University libraries are for the serious study of these subjects by students and faculty. They are not convenience stores frequented by browsing children. And those students and faculty who would learn or teach the origins of the Second World War, for example, must be able to understand the Nazi leader who played the key part in plunging the world into that war.

If uncomfortable questions lead to new knowledge based on solid research, so be it. Scholars who take issue with the research or the conclusions have a duty to challenge the new knowledge they do not like through research and publication of their own. They must not simply denounce such work as being unacceptable on a university campus. To do so is to attack the very foundations of free inquiry and, indeed, of the university itself.

Such an attack is happening with increasing frequency. One current example is the work being done by a handful of scholars on whether a phenomenon known as suppressed memory exists. Individuals who come forward in later life to claim gross sexual abuse as children often attribute the tardiness of their claims to suppressed memory. Personality disorders of certain types are sometimes attributed to these suppressed memories, which are often linked to ritualistic devil-worship practices. Yet when charges are brought against those who are accused of the sexual abuse, there are many cases where no evidence whatever can be found to support the claim. Do such suppressed memories actually exist, then?

A number of scholars have conducted research into the phenomenon and concluded that it does not. Others have come to opposite conclusions. For some extremists on campus, however, the subject is much more than a debate among scientists; it is nothing less than a political plot mounted by one group of scholars to discredit sexually abused women, and a crusade from the opposing side to protect women's interests. Some of the leading proponents of the idea that suppressed memory is a myth have been loudly shouted down from lecture podiums. Their science is politically unacceptable to one small element of a university society, which then denies them the right to speak freely and without harassment about the research they do. Those are Nazi-style tactics and they menace the very idea of a university. Some professors, including women, who disagree with gender-based hiring quotas have been treated similarly. So have teachers who have dared not to include this or that approach in courses on lesbian literature.

Where will all this end? Should universities stop teaching business courses, for example, because some scholars claim that business exploits workers? Or should history professors avoid teaching about wars because war is brutal and nasty? Should the great classics on which Western civilization is based be ignored because they were, almost without exception, written by dead white males? To ask the question is to answer with a resounding no. That does not mean that universities should not evolve to reflect new discoveries, new areas of research, new knowledge. We have no doubt that Canadian students have much to learn from feminist writers, from Chinese philosophers, from African-American political scientists — indeed, from all manner of peoples whose experiences are different from ours. But we also believe that adding new knowledge must never become a zero-sum game, even if curricula are, as they must be, restricted by numbers and budgets.

Some of Canada's better universities live by this inclusive approach, and we commend them as the best places to get an undergraduate education. We won't provide a shopping list of which universities to consider and which not, but we believe that some universities do offer a better undergraduate education and that there are specific things to look for when trying to choose a graduate school. The great secret that few universities care to talk about is that at *this* stage in the development of higher education in Canada, all but a few publicly funded universities are pretty much the same in the quality of undergraduate education they offer.

———

The most important thing to look for in a Canadian university today is that it offers a good mix of both graduate and undergraduate programs. It will then be a well-balanced institution where solid undergraduate teaching, along with research and graduate studies, receives priority. The researchers should be doing a fair share of the undergraduate teaching, not just teaching assistants or laboratory demonstrators. A large part of the first-year teaching should also be performed by the university's best lecturers. Most universities today survey undergraduate students each year to test the quality of the content and the teaching of their courses. Prospective students should look at these results and ask department heads about their priorities. If students are not satisfied, they should find another university.

Equally important is the university's philosophy in forming and delivering its undergraduate curriculum. Is there broad choice? Will students be obliged to dip into different disciplines to gain some knowledge of, say, mathematics, English literature, philosophy, or the scientific method? Is the scope of the program broad enough in the first two years to awaken interest in subjects that students may never have encountered before? Are there honours programs? Do they require students to maintain a high grade point average? They should! Will the department of choice allow students to take courses from other disciplines? Is the department enthusiastic about cross- or multi-disciplinary work, or will it in fact erect substantial bureaucratic barriers against such innovative approaches?

Finally, how good are the majors and the honours programs and how well will they prepare students for their next step, whatever that will be? Are the libraries supporting these senior programs up to date? Are the electronic supports — the computers, servers, networks — of the highest calibre? Are the professors applying new knowledge gained through research directly into the classroom? Are the professors in these senior courses doing worthwhile research at all? How can students find out before they enrol? They should take the names of these potential professors and run them through the library's computer or through one of a number of periodical indexes available on CD-ROM to find out if each one has an active research and publishing career. Or they can ask to see a particular professor's curriculum vitae.

Graduate schools are more easily chosen. The two most important things students should look for are the ratio of supervisors to students in the particular department or discipline of interest and the amount of research being carried out. The former figure should be easily obtainable from the graduate faculty or the department. The lower the ratio, the better. More important, the potential graduate student should find out how many other graduate students a particular supervisor is responsible for at the time. Any supervisor who is working with eight or more students should be avoided. The higher the number, the higher the drop-out rate is likely to be and the longer it is likely to take a student to get the degree. Graduate students *need* personal attention. Graduate education is primarily about *mentoring*. Students won't get that attention or that mentoring if they are just one of a crowd.

To get a feel for the scope and depth of the research being done by the professors they want to work with, graduate students should ask about their potential supervisors' recent publications or for a list of recent research grants and/or contracts awarded to those supervisors or that department. A graduate education will cost the student and the taxpayer quite a bit, so students should make sure that the money is well spent. They should also ask their own undergraduate instructors who they think might be good graduate supervisors.

If students are interested in university teaching, they should think long and hard about the gamble they are about to take. There is some demand for new university teachers in certain disciplines, almost none in others. If students have a genuine interest in a discipline where few university jobs are likely to open up soon (in the next five years or so), they should not think that they will necessarily be the lucky ones to snare the few jobs that may be open. There will be hundreds of others who will think the same. If students want to take a graduate degree in history, for example, they can enjoy the history learning experience but should not expect to get a job any time soon. They should go into it with their eyes wide open and not complain if they fail to find that tenure-track job they thought they would get.

Our best advice to students is simple: Don't be swayed by major brand names. The top of the *Maclean's* list isn't necessarily the best place to start looking for a good university. Students who live in Fredericton, for example, will find one of Canada's best programs in security studies and military history at the local university. Those who live in Regina will have easy access to one of the most advanced globalization programs in the country. We could go on, but the point is simple. A university may be rated as Canada's "best" university in this or that category, but that does not mean that all of its programs are the best.

When we concluded *The Great Brain Robbery* over a decade ago, we exhorted, "Let *something* be done, quickly!" Much has been done; Canadian universities *are* better now than they were then. But universities have been around for about a thousand years and the process of adoption and improvement must be constant. No matter how flexible universities become in their delivery methods, or how current in some of their subject matter, their aim must remain the same: teaching and learning, in a spirit of free inquiry, with the object of bringing human minds to their full potential.

Index

influence on Canada, 13-14, 17,
32, 45
private universities, 32-33
recruitment of Canadians for distance
education, 82, 83
salaries of professors in, 36-37
state schools, 33
tuition fees in, 31, 189, 201
University of Alberta, 38, 50-51, 135
University of British Columbia, 35, 63,
195, 196
academic freedom policy, 140
quotas, 123
unverified accusations, 91, 113-21
University of Calgary, 55, 58, 60, 71, 83,
135, 138
University du Québec à Montréal, 60
University of Hawaii, 150-51
University of Manitoba, 55, 104, 135
University of Michigan, 36-37
University of New Brunswick, 56, 154
punishment of Yaqzan, 99-101
University of Ottawa, 48
University of Pennsylvania, 36
University presses, 166-70, 173, 174-75
University of Regina, 63
University of Saskatchewan, 63
University teaching, 80-82, 207-8
University of Toronto, 31, 36, 38, 40, 81,
181, 195, 196
dismissal case, 138-39
"political correctness" officers, 103-4
University of Victoria:
planning at, 71-72
unsubstantiated harassment claims at,
111-13
University of Waterloo, 38-39, 53, 64

University of Western Ontario, 31, 38, 64,
84, 104
and criticism of Rushton, 97, 98, 147
University of Winnipeg, 55
Upper Canada College (private high
school), 60-61

Veterans in universities, 13
Vickers, Jill, 105-8
Video conferencing, 76

Weir, Lorna, 92
Welfare state, 16-17
Wente, Margaret, 116
Wilfrid Laurier University, 134
Wilson, Justice Bertha, 144
Women:
professors, 21-22, 93, 105-8, 122-23,
126, 150, 203
students, 22, 68, 105-6, 121-22, 182, 203
World Wide Web, 72, 77

Yaqzan, Matin, 99-101, 130
York University, 64, 103, 122, 134, 138,
139-40, 146
Atkinson College, 86

"Zero-tolerance" against discrimination,
102-3, 104, 105, 110-11